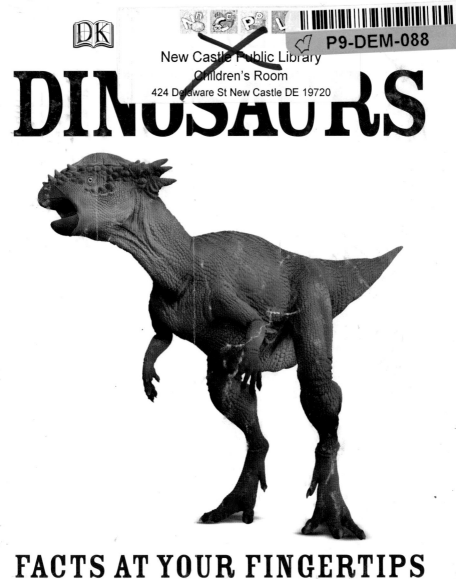

DK

# DINOSAURS

# FACTS AT YOUR FINGERTIPS

LONDON, NEW YORK, MUNICH,
MELBOURNE, and DELHI

**DK DELHI**
**Project editor** Virien Chopra
**Project art editor** Nishesh Batnagar
**Senior editor** Kingshuk Ghoshal
**Senior art editor** Govind Mittal
**Art editor** Isha Nagar
**DTP designers** Mohammad Usman, Vishal Bhatia
**Picture researcher** Sumedha Chopra
**Managing editor** Saloni Talwar
**Managing art editor** Romi Chakraborty
**CTS manager** Balwant Singh
**Production manager** Pankaj Sharma

**DK LONDON**
**Senior editor** Dr. Rob Houston
**Senior art editor** Philip Letsu
**US editor** Margaret Parrish
**Jacket editor** Manisha Majithia
**Jacket designer** Laura Brim
**Jacket design development manager**
Sophia Tampakopolous
**Production editor** Ben Marcus
**Production controller** Mary Slater

**Publisher** Andrew Macintyre
**Associate publishing director** Liz Wheeler
**Art director** Phil Ormerod
**Publishing director** Jonathan Metcalf

**Consultant** Professor Michael J. Benton

First published in the United States in 2012
by DK Publishing
375 Hudson Street, New York, New York 10014

Copyright © 2012 Dorling Kindersley Limited
12 13 14 15 16  10 9 8 7 6 5 4 3 2 1
001–182432–Jun/12

A catalog record for this book
is available from the Library of Congress.

ISBN: 978-0-7566-9315-2

Printed and bound by South China
Printing Company, China

**Discover more at
www.dk.com**

# CONTENTS

**Scales and sizes**
This book contains profiles of
prehistoric animals with scale
drawings to indicate their size.

6 ft
(1.8 m)

7 in
(18 cm)

*Kentrosaurus*

# Before the dinosaurs

The Earth is more than 4.5 billion years old, and the first traces of life appeared some 1 billion years after it formed. Single-celled organisms were the first life-forms to appear, and over millions of years they evolved into invertebrates (animals without backbones) and vertebrates (animals with backbones). The Earth's history is divided into eras, which are further divided into periods.

## Cambrian Explosion

Around 530 million years ago (mya), there was a rapid increase in the number of different kinds of invertebrate animals. This is known as the Cambrian Explosion, because it occurred in the Cambrian Period.

*Anomalocaris*, one of the top predators of the Cambrian oceans

| PRECAMBRIAN | Cambrian | Ordovician | Silurian |
|---|---|---|---|
| | PALEOZOIC ERA | | |
| | 542 mya | 488 mya | 443 mya |

## Precambrian life

Some of the first living organisms were bacteria living in mats on the seabed. They trapped sand and used it to build rocky mounds called stromatolites, just as some still do today (left). Some fossil stromatolites are an incredible 3.5 million years old.

Stromatolites

# Devonian plants

The Devonian Period lasted from 416 to 359 mya. It was in this period that the plant *Archaeopteris* appeared. It was the first tree to form dense forests that spread across the planet.

*Dimetrodon*

# Permian reptiles

Many different reptile groups were widespread in the Permian Period, including ancestors of the dinosaurs. *Dimetrodon*, however, was a remote ancestor of mammals.

*Archaeopteris*

| Devonian | Carboniferous | Permian |
|---|---|---|

299 mya

252 mya

*Amphibamus*

# Carboniferous amphibians

First appearing in the Devonian Period, four-legged vertebrates, or tetrapods, were common on land by the Carboniferous Period. The amphibian *Amphibamus* was an early tetrapod.

# Dinosaurs and after

The dinosaurs lived in the Mesozoic Era, which lasted from 252 to 65 mya. This era is further divided into the Triassic, Jurassic, and Cretaceous periods. The dinosaurs died out at the end of the Cretaceous Period, around 65 mya. The earliest hominids (members of the human family) appeared around 4.4 mya.

## First dinosaurs

Dinosaurs first evolved in the Triassic Period. Early dinosaurs were small, two-legged animals, such as *Eoraptor*.

*Eoraptor*

| Triassic | Jurassic |
|----------|----------|

**MESOZOIC ERA**

252 mya

200 mya

## Jurassic giants

Dinosaurs continued to evolve in the Jurassic, and became the dominant life-forms on land. Some grew to huge sizes, such as the sauropods, while others, such as the theropod *Archaeopteryx,* took to the air.

*Mamenchisaurus,*
*a sauropod*

## Primates emerge

The era after the Mesozoic is called the Cenozoic Era. It contains the Paleogene Period, in which primates, the mammalian ancestors of humans, first appeared.

## Coming of humans

Many modern mammals, including horses, camels, and cows, evolved in the Neogene period. Hominids—the ancestors of humans—appeared in Africa and spread across the world.

*Eosimias,* an early primate

| Cretaceous | Paleogene | Neogene |
|---|---|---|
| | CENOZOIC ERA | |
| | 65 mya | 23 mya |

## Present day

We live in what is called the Quaternary Period, which started 2.6 mya and continues to the present day.

## Dinosaurs die out

The Cretaceous Period saw the emergence of new types of dinosaur, including the horned ceratopsians and armored ankylosaurs. Around 65 mya, an asteroid or comet collided with the Earth, killing off the dinosaurs and marking the end of the Mesozoic Era.

# The Triassic

Pangaea
Pangaea

The Triassic Period lasted from 252 mya to 200 mya. During this period, the Earth's continents were joined together as a single landmass called Pangaea. Just before the Triassic, a mass extinction had wiped out a vast number of life-forms, including most land animals. The empty habitats began to be filled by a range of reptiles and eventually, the first dinosaurs. Mammals also appeared at this time.

*Pleuromeia*

## A changing world

Deserts spanned the globe during the Triassic, and most plants grew near coasts and in river valleys, where the soil was moist. Ferns and treelike plants, such as *Pleuromeia,* flourished during this time.

**Fern frond**

## Early fliers

Some reptiles took to the air for the first time during the Triassic. These were the pterosaurs, which were close relatives of the dinosaurs.

*Eudimorphodon*,
an early pterosaur

*Hyperodapedon*,
a rhynchosaur

## Plant-eaters

Large animals that roamed the land during the Triassic included the rhynchosaurs, a group of piglike, plant-eating reptiles.

## Dinosaurs

The earliest known dinosaurs, such as *Coelophysis*, appeared in the Triassic, some 230 mya. Most dinosaurs of this time were small, about the height of a man, and greatly outnumbered by other reptiles.

*Coelophysis*

# The Jurassic

The Jurassic Period started around 200 mya, and lasted for 54 million years. Around 175 mya, Pangaea began breaking up into two large continents—Laurasia and Gondwana, as seen on the left. Scientists believe that a mass extinction at the start of the Jurassic wiped out most of the non-dinosaur reptiles of the Triassic. This reduced the competition for food and allowed dinosaurs to flourish.

Laurasia

Laurasia

Atlantic Ocean

Gondwana

## Sea monsters

During the Mesozoic Era, the seas were ruled by giant reptiles. In the Jurassic, these included the dolphinlike ichthyosaurs and the lizardlike plesiosaurs.

*Ichthyosaurus*, an ichthyosaur

## A new environment

The Triassic deserts transformed into lush green forests, filled with plants that had developed in the Triassic. These included coniferous trees, such as the monkey puzzle—a plant still present today—and *Williamsonia*, a small tree with palmlike fronds.

*Williamsonia*

**Leaves of a monkey puzzle tree**

## Flying aces

The pterosaurs of the Triassic evolved into the more efficient fliers of the Jurassic, such as *Pterodactylus*. This pterosaur had longer wings and a shorter tail, making it more agile in the air.

**Pterodactylus**

## The age of giants

The colossal sauropods were the largest creatures ever to walk on the Earth, some of them reaching up to 59 ft (18 m) in height. These giants thundered through the forests in herds and they were often preyed upon by the largest theropods—ferocious meat-eating dinosaurs.

**Brachiosaurus, a sauropod**

# The Cretaceous

Lasting from 145 mya until 65 mya, the Cretaceous Period saw a number of changes across the globe. Laurasia and Gondwana broke up and began taking on the positions and shapes of continents today. The sauropods began to decline in number, while other plant-eaters, such as the duck-billed dinosaurs and ceratopsians, flourished. Flowering plants also began appearing in this period.

North America

Eurasia

Africa

South America

Antarctica

## Adding color

In the Early Cretaceous, lush green forests of conifers and ferns still covered most of the land. One plant of the time was the tree-fern *Tempskya*. Instead of a trunk, it had a number of shoots joined together. Eventually, the landscape began to change. Flowering plants, such as magnolia, appeared, adding color to the vegetation.

*Tempskya*

**Magnolia flower**

## Feathered fliers

Although the first birds evolved in the Jurassic, those that appeared in the Cretaceous were more varied. Some had toothless beaks and other features similar to today's birds.

*Liaoxiornis,*
**an early bird**

*Mosasaurus,*
**a mosasaur**

*Zalambdalestes*

## Little scavengers

Mammals lived throughout the age of the dinosaurs, but remained small, feeding on plants, small animals, and eggs.

## Ambush predators

During the Cretaceous, the oceans were ruled by gigantic predators called mosasaurs. Their powerful tails made them good swimmers, but these giants preferred to lie in wait before pouncing on their prey, rather than chasing it down.

## Jungle grazer

Ceratopsians, along with duck-billed dinosaurs, such as *Maiasaura,* became widespread in the Cretaceous. *Triceratops* was a large plant-eating ceratopsian that lived in herds, probably feeding on flowering plants.

*Triceratops*

# Dinosaur ancestors

Dinosaurs, like all land animals with backbones, evolved from fish. The fins of the fish developed into limbs that helped in walking on land, while lungs developed and allowed breathing. One group of these animals evolved into the reptiles, and some reptiles evolved into dinosaurs.

*Panderichthys*

## First steps

*Acanthostega* was one of the earliest tetrapods. It had a fishlike tail fin that pushed it through the water, and four limbs, each with eight toes, which allowed it to walk.

Paddlelike tail fin

Leg with eight **toelike** digits

*Acanthostega*

## Fishy bones

Lobe-finned fish, such as *Panderichthys*, were the ancestors of all four-legged backboned animals, or tetrapods. Their fins sprouted from fleshy structures, or lobes, strengthened by bones like those in our limbs.

## Protecting the eggs

The eggs of early tetrapods needed to be laid in water. Over time, some tetrapods, such as *Westlothiana*, evolved eggs with a waterproof membrane. This allowed them to lay their eggs on land, and the eggs didn't dry out. These animals began breeding on land, evolving into reptiles, dinosaurs, and mammals.

*Westlothiana*

**Bony plates** along back

**Sideways** facing eyes

# Dinosaur cousins

Dinosaurs are part of a group of reptiles called archosaurs. Modern crocodiles also belong to this group and evolved from early archosaurs, such as *Parasuchus*. The early archosaurs moved with their knees bent, giving them a sprawling walk.

*Parasuchus*

**Sprawling** front limbs

*Postosuchus*, an advanced archosaur

# On two legs

As archosaurs evolved, some began to stand upright, and unlike the sprawling legs of crocodiles, their legs supported the body high above the ground, allowing agile and efficient running. Scientists believe that dinosaurs may have evolved from these kinds of upright archosaurs.

# Types of dinosaur

More than 1,000 species of dinosaur lived in the Mesozoic. Enormous sauropods grazed on the very tops of trees, while packs of meat-eating theropods chased down their prey and ripped it apart with sharp teeth and claws. Some dinosaurs had armored skins, while others had horns or spikes to protect themselves.

## Huge!

Some dinosaurs were the largest animals ever to walk on the Earth, but no one is sure why they grew so big. Some scientists suggest size developed as a defense against predators. Others propose that an abundance of food led to these giants.

*Barosaurus*, a sauropod, length 92 ft (28 m)

*Muttaburrasaurus*, an ornithopod, length 26 ft (8 m)

*Ankylosaurus*, an ankylosaur, length 20 ft (6 m)

# Dinosaurs

## Family tree

Early dinosaurs evolved into two main groups—the ornithischians and the saurischians. Saurischians include the meat-eating theropods and the long-necked sauropodomorphs—a large group containing the sauropods and prosauropods. Ornithischians also branched into different types. The armored ankylosaurs and stegosaurs broke off first, with the three-toed ornithopods and frilled ceratopsians and pachycephalosaurs appearing later.

Saurischians

Ornithischians

Theropods

Sauropodomorphs

Ankylosaurs

Stegosaurs

Ornithopods

Pachycephalosaurs

Ceratopsians

*Styracosaurus*, a ceratopsian, length 17 ft (5.2 m)

*Alxasaurus*, a theropod, length 13 ft (4 m)

Modern man, average height 6 ft (1.8 m)

# Dinosaurs to birds

We now know that birds evolved from theropod dinosaurs. However, the features that define modern birds—flight feathers, short tails, and a curved breastbone with strong flight muscles that allow them to fly—were not present in their theropod ancestors. It took millions of years for these features to appear.

## Feathered find

When it was first discovered in 1996, *Sinosauropteryx* caused a huge sensation among scientists. It had a soft, fuzzy covering that resembled feathers. Scientists realized that dinosaurs evolved feathers before taking to the air.

## Using feathers

The first feathers were not used for flight. Some feathers helped keep the theropods warm, while others were used for display. We know this because of the well-preserved fossils of *Sinornithosaurus*, which show remains of feathers of various kinds.

A complete fossil of *Sinornithosaurus*

## Micro flier

One of the smallest dinosaurs, *Microraptor* was slightly bigger than a pigeon. This tiny theropod had asymmetrical feathers on its arms and legs that generated lift, allowing it to glide from tree to tree.

## First bird

Once considered the first true bird, *Archaeopteryx* is one of the earliest known theropods capable of weakly powered flight. Its asymmetrical feathers also allowed it to glide. This Jurassic dinosaur, however, still had a long reptilelike tail and claws on its wings.

## Modern bird

*Iberomesornis* was a finch-sized creature that lived in the Cretaceous and was one of the many birds that gave rise to modern birds. It had a short tail with tail feathers, and a curved breastbone, but lacked the strong flight muscles of modern birds.

## EVOLUTION OF FEATHERS

**Hollow** hairlike filaments were the first feathers.

**Tufted** barbs joined at the base developed from the single filaments.

**Barbs** connected to a central axis developed next.

**Asymmetrical** feathers evolved. These could provide lift for flying.

# Dinosaurs die out

The dinosaurs dominated the Earth for more than 160 million years. Then, about 65 mya, they disappeared in a mass extinction of many life-forms. There are many theories about why dinosaurs died out. The strongest evidence shows that an asteroid or comet crashed into the Earth. At the same time, volcanoes erupted. Both events led to drastic climate change.

## Death from the skies

Scientists know that an asteroid or comet, 6 miles (10 km) across, collided with the Earth at a very high speed. The impact threw up huge quantities of dust into the air, blocking out the Sun. Without the Sun's heat, temperatures across the Earth dropped rapidly, and most life-forms perished. This coincided with an increase in volcanic activity. Erupting volcanoes would have released large amounts of ash and toxic gases, destroying animal and plant life.

## EVIDENCE

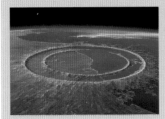

**Deep impact** Scientists know that the Chicxulub crater in the Yucatán Peninsula of Mexico was made by an asteroid or comet impact 65 mya. This artistic depiction shows how the impact crater might have looked from space. The crater was discovered in the 1990s and is more than 110 miles (180 km) across.

**Volcanic activity** This mass of rock is the Deccan Traps in India. It was formed by lava flow. One of the largest volcanic features on the Earth, it was built up by a series of volcanic eruptions 80 to 60 mya. It is estimated that the lava flow covered an area of 580,000 sq miles (1.5 million sq km)—half the size of modern India.

*Phenacodus,*
**a mammal that lived in the Paleogene**

## Survivors

The survivors of the mass extinction included birds and the small, shrewlike mammals of the Cretaceous. With the theropods dead, there were no major predators left, and these mammals flourished, growing larger and becoming widespread.

# How fossils form

Nearly everything we know about dinosaurs we learn from fossils. Fossils are the remains or traces of plants and animals that have actually turned to rock over millions of years. The rock usually forms as mineral-rich water trickles into the tiny spaces inside bones, shells, or tree trunks.

## Fossilized

An animal only turns into a fossil when it dies if a few lucky things happen together. First, it must be buried quickly—perhaps by wind-blown sand or river mud. Over the millennia, the animal's skeleton changes into rock, or leaves an impression on the surrounding rock.

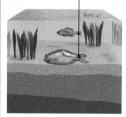

Decaying body

1. **A fish sinks** to the riverbed when it dies. Its soft parts might rot or be eaten.

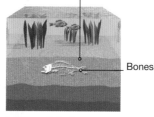

Sediments such as sand or mud build over skeleton

Bones

2. **Minerals** in the water may seep into the tiny spaces in the bone and crystallize.

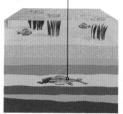

Layers of sediment squash fossil

3. **With time,** heat, and pressure, the mineral crystals in the bones turn into rock.

Fossilized fish skeleton

Rock exposed due to erosion by wind and water

4. **Over millions of years,** the layers of rock above may be worn away, leaving the skeleton at the Earth's surface—ready for fossil hunters to discover.

## Mineral invasion

Ammonites were squidlike creatures that lived inside a coiled shell. They existed at the same time as the dinosaurs. The spaces inside this ammonite's fossil shell have been filled with a mineral called pyrite, also known as fool's gold. The shell itself has been transformed into a darker mineral.

## Soft parts preserved

Usually, only hard parts of an animal, such as shell and bone, are fossilized, because soft parts are eaten or rot away before they are buried. In rare cases of a very quick burial, skin and other soft parts can be preserved as rock.

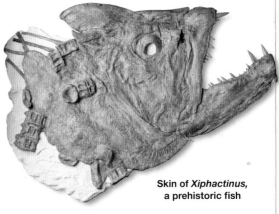

**Skin of *Xiphactinus*, a prehistoric fish**

## Trace fossils

Fossils are not always the remains of animal and plant bodies. They can be marks and signs they left behind, such as eggs, droppings, and footprints. These signs are called trace fossils.

**Model of *Allosaurus* and *Apatosaurus* footprints**

# Fossil bones

Whole skeletons are rarely discovered intact. Most fossils are single teeth, bones, or partial skeletons. Paleontologists must use this scant evidence to piece together the missing parts. Sometimes, fossil hunters are lucky enough to find whole skeletons, some of which are even still "articulated" (all bones in place).

## Iguanodon hand fossil

A thumb spike can be clearly seen in this nicely articulated *Iguanodon* fossil, but scientists have not always had such good evidence of this animal. *Iguanodon* was one of the first dinosaurs to be discovered. In 1820, English doctor Gideon Mantell found fossil teeth in a quarry and realized that they belonged to a giant prehistoric animal. Soon afterward, Mantell and others found more nonarticulated *Iguanodon* bones. Limited fossil evidence was easy to misinterpret. In piecing together the creature, Mantell mistakenly placed the thumb spike as a horn on its nose!

Hand bone

Spike on thumb

| | |
|---|---|
| **DATE** | 135–125 mya (Early Cretaceous) |
| **SIZE** | 10 in (25 cm) long |
| **FOSSIL LOCATION** | England |
| **ANIMAL GROUP** | Dinosaurs |

## Gryposaurus skeleton

*Gryposaurus* was a hadrosaur (see pp. 92–93). This skeleton was found in Alberta, Canada, at a site called the Dinosaur Park Formation. It is partially embedded in rock and partially mounted. Scientists mount such complete fossil specimens based on their understanding of how the creature stood and moved. Intact fossils such as this show that strong tendons held up the tail, preventing it from sagging. Earlier reconstructions of these creatures pictured them standing upright.

*Tendons helped to stiffen tail*

| | |
|---|---|
| **DATE** | 83–75 mya (Late Cretaceous) |
| **SIZE** | 29½ ft (9 m) long |
| **FOSSIL LOCATION** | North America |
| **ANIMAL GROUP** | Dinosaurs |

## Baryonyx claw fossil

Scientists don't know for certain if this *Baryonyx* claw came from its index finger or thumb. Fossils of single claws found separated from the body can be misleading. The claw had a groove where a sheath of horn was attached.

| | |
|---|---|
| **DATE** | 125 mya (Early Cretaceous) |
| **SIZE** | 14 in (35 cm) from tip to base |
| **FOSSIL LOCATION** | England |
| **ANIMAL GROUP** | Dinosaurs |

## Gallimimus skull fossil

*Gallimimus* had a birdlike skull with a long toothless beak. It had wide eye sockets with eyes facing sideways. Each eyeball was supported by a ring of bony plates.

| | |
|---|---|
| **DATE** | 75–65 mya (Late Cretaceous) |
| **SIZE** | 12 in (30 cm) long |
| **FOSSIL LOCATION** | Mongolia |
| **ANIMAL GROUP** | Dinosaurs |

# Exceptional fossils

The hard parts of an animal's body tend to fossilize the best. In exceptional cases, however, an animal might be buried rapidly with no chance for the soft body parts to rot. The resulting fossils include those of skin and feathers, and even internal organs.

## Edmontosaurus skin fossil

Mud filled every crease in the skin of *Edmontosaurus* to create this fine fossil, called a cast, which shows what the scales on the skin looked like.

| | |
|---|---|
| **DATE** | 75–65 mya (Late Cretaceous) |
| **SIZE** | 8 in (20 cm) across |
| **FOSSIL LOCATION** | United States |
| **ANIMAL GROUP** | Dinosaurs |

## Polacanthus skin fossil

This *Polacanthus* fossil has traces of the animal's knobby skin. Mud covered the animal before its body had decayed and a mold (impression) of its skin was filled by the mud. This turned to rock, preserving the spiked lumps on the skin of this ankylosaur.

*Large, spiked lump*

| | |
|---|---|
| **DATE** | 130 mya (Early Cretaceous) |
| **SIZE** | 6 in (15 cm) across |
| **FOSSIL LOCATION** | England |
| **ANIMAL GROUP** | Dinosaurs |

# Sinornithosaurus fossil

In 2001, paleontologists discovered this complete fossil of *Sinornithosaurus* in China. Impressions of primitive feathers line the bones of this creature. This dinosaur was a ground-dwelling animal and probably died on a riverbed with a fish in its claws. It was buried so quickly that its feathers were intact and left their shapes on the surrounding mud before rotting away. This discovery helped scientists understand that not all kinds of feather were used for flying. Some kinds helped keep the feathered theropods warm.

Feather impression

Fossil fish

**DATE** 130–125 mya (Early Cretaceous)

**SIZE** 3¼ ft (1 m) long

**FOSSIL LOCATION** China

**ANIMAL GROUP** Dinosaurs

*Sinornithosaurus* means "Chinese bird lizard," but this creature was not a true bird and couldn't fly.

# Trace fossils

Sometimes an animal leaves behind a hint, or trace, of its presence. The remains of such traces of prehistoric creatures and their activities, preserved in rock, are called trace fossils. These include footprints, bite marks, droppings, and eggs.

## Ichthyosaur coprolite

Coprolites are the fossilized dung of prehistoric creatures. Scientists study these fossil droppings to understand more about the diets of the animals. This is the coprolite of a marine reptile called an ichthyosaur (see pp. 124–25). Undigested scraps of bone and shell from its last meal can reveal the kinds of prey it fed on.

| | |
|---|---|
| **DATE** | 190 mya (Early Jurassic) |
| **SIZE** | 3¼ in (8 cm) long |
| **FOSSIL LOCATION** | England |
| **ANIMAL GROUP** | Ichthyosaurs |

## Apatosaurus egg fossil

This is a fossilized egg of the sauropod *Apatosaurus* (see pp. 60–61). The eggs of sauropods had a thick shell that protected them from breakage. The eggs seem small in comparision to the sizes of these giants, but larger eggs would have needed shells so thick that hatchlings could not have broken out.

| | |
|---|---|
| **DATE** | 154–150 mya (Late Jurassic) |
| **SIZE** | 5 in (13 cm) across |
| **FOSSIL LOCATION** | United States |
| **ANIMAL GROUP** | Dinosaurs |

## Oviraptor egg and embryo fossils

These are the fossilized bones of an embryo of the theropod *Oviraptor*. They lie within the fossil remains of an egg shell and were found in a fossilized nest in the Gobi Desert. Finding the delicate bones of an embryo like this helps scientists figure out which dinosaur laid the eggs.

| | |
|---|---|
| **DATE** | 75 mya (Late Cretaceous) |
| **SIZE** | 7 in (18 cm) long |
| **FOSSIL LOCATION** | Mongolia |
| **ANIMAL GROUP** | Dinosaurs |

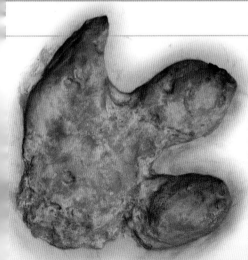

## Iguanodon footprint

A young *Iguanodon* left this footprint in the Early Cretaceous. Sometimes footprints get preserved in layers of mud, which hardens to rock, in turn preserving the footprints as fossils. The shapes and sizes of these prints and the gaps between them allow scientists to identify the kinds of dinosaur that made the prints, and also to figure out the sizes of the dinosaurs and how fast they walked or ran. Based on the length of this footprint, scientists determined that it was made by an *Iguanodon* weighing roughly half a ton.

| | |
|---|---|
| **DATE** | 135–125 mya (Early Cretaceous) |
| **SIZE** | 11½ in (29 cm) long |
| **FOSSIL LOCATION** | England |
| **ANIMAL GROUP** | Dinosaurs |

# Reconstruction

Reconstructing dinosaurs requires a lot of research. After excavating fossils, scientists study them and compare them to modern reptiles to understand how the bones in a dinosaur skeleton connected to each other and to the muscles that moved a dinosaur's body.

## Mounting dinosaurs

When arranging a dinosaur skeleton, scientists not only have to make sure of how the bones connect, but they also have to fix the dinosaur's pose. Sometimes, new research leads to resetting of the posture. For example, it was once thought that sauropods dragged their tails on the ground, but we now know that they held their tails aloft.

# Let's move

Dinosaurs can be re-created as moving 3-D digital models using CGI, or computer-generated imagery. This is how the *Corythosaurus* image (p. 93) was built.

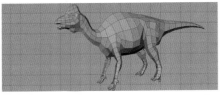

1. Scientists and computer programmers study the dinosaur's bones and make a basic model from geometrical shapes on a computer. This is called a wireframe.

2. A computer program divides the geometrical figures into millions of smaller units. An artist can then shape each unit, refining the dinosaur's shape.

3. New discoveries about the dinosaur, such as the size and shape of its crest, are added to the sculpture. This helps create an accurate model of the dinosaur.

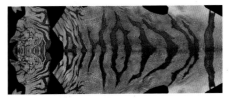

4. Adding color to the dinosaur involves a mix of artistic creativity and scientific insight. Fossil dinosaur skin may feature intact microscopic pigment capsules, the shapes of which help scientists deduce the dinosaur's color.

5. A rigger (a specialized programmer with expertise in anatomy) tells the computer how the different parts of the body would have moved.

6. Scientists tell the artist what kind of environment the dinosaur lived in, allowing the artist to create realistic backgrounds of the dinosaur's habitat.

# Dinosaurs

Dinosaurs were the dominant land animals for more than 160 million years and ranged from small animals no bigger than pigeons to lumbering giants the size of a truck. As scientists have studied remains of these ancient reptiles, they have found evidence of the original colors of these creatures in their feathers. Many dinosaurs had striped or bright feathers, and probably also multicolored skin, feathers, frills, and head crests, which made them look more attractive or fierce.

**JURASSIC FOREST**
Thick, lush forest covered the land during the Jurassic, with trees and ferns providing food and shelter for the dinosaurs.

# The first dinosaurs

Dinosaurs evolved in the Triassic Period. The earliest ones were agile animals that walked on their hind legs and had sharp teeth and claws. Many of them were omnivores that fed on a variety of foods. They gradually evolved into specialized plant-eating and meat-eating dinosaurs.

## Herrerasaurus
her-air-ah-SORE-us

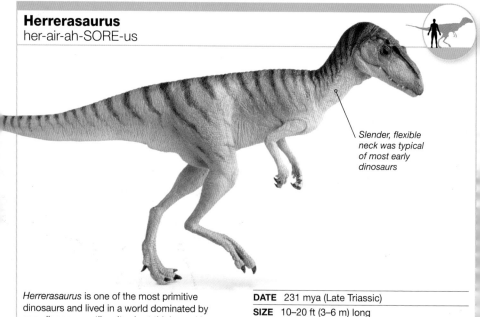

*Slender, flexible neck was typical of most early dinosaurs*

*Herrerasaurus* is one of the most primitive dinosaurs and lived in a world dominated by non-dinosaur reptiles. Its short thighs and long feet made it a fast runner, like most of the earliest dinosaurs, and it could probably have easily outrun its prey.

| | |
|---|---|
| **DATE** | 231 mya (Late Triassic) |
| **SIZE** | 10–20 ft (3–6 m) long |
| **FOSSIL LOCATION** | Argentina |
| **HABITAT** | Forests |
| **DIET** | Animals |

## Eoraptor
ee-oh-RAP-ter

One of the earliest saurischians, *Eoraptor* was the size of a fox. It had the sawlike teeth of a hunter. Its eyes faced toward the side.

**DATE** 231 mya (Late Triassic)

**SIZE** 3¼ ft (1 m) long

**FOSSIL LOCATION** Argentina

**HABITAT** Forests

**DIET** Lizards, small reptiles, and plants

## Eocursor
ee-oh-CUR-ser

*Eocursor* was an early ornithischian. This omnivore could run quickly on its hind legs. Its hands were armed with sharp claws that probably helped in catching small animals.

**DATE** 210 mya (Late Triassic)

**SIZE** 3¼ ft (1 m) long

**FOSSIL LOCATION** South Africa

**HABITAT** Moist forests

**DIET** Plants, small mammals, and reptiles

## Gojirasaurus
go-JEER-a-SORE-us

The movie monster Godzilla, known as *Gojira* in Japanese, inspired the name of this meat-eater. It prowled across the arid regions of what is now North America, and it was the top predator of the American Southwest.

**DATE** 210 mya (Late Triassic)

**SIZE** 16½–23 ft (5–7 m) long

**FOSSIL LOCATION** United States

**HABITAT** Scrublands

**DIET** Animals

## JAW DIVERSITY

The jaws of theropods were suited to catching and eating in different ways.

▲ *Baryonyx* had narrow jaws with pointed teeth, good for catching fish.

▲ *Deinonychus* had pointed jaws, good for tearing out pieces of flesh.

▲ *Tyrannosaurus* had big, U-shaped jaws, which tore out large chunks of meat.

# Theropods

A varied group, theropods included all predatory dinosaurs, some omnivores, and probably some plant-eaters. Some predatory theropods were tiny, some were birdlike, and others were giant top predators. They killed prey with bladelike teeth and sharp claws.

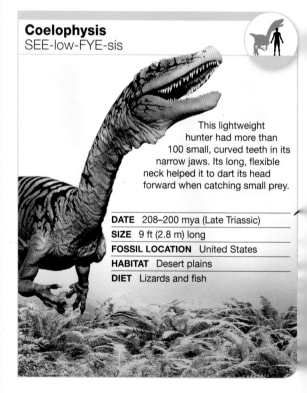

### Coelophysis
SEE-low-FYE-sis

This lightweight hunter had more than 100 small, curved teeth in its narrow jaws. Its long, flexible neck helped it to dart its head forward when catching small prey.

| | |
|---|---|
| **DATE** | 208–200 mya (Late Triassic) |
| **SIZE** | 9 ft (2.8 m) long |
| **FOSSIL LOCATION** | United States |
| **HABITAT** | Desert plains |
| **DIET** | Lizards and fish |

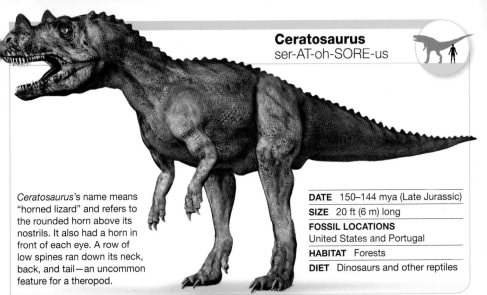

# Ceratosaurus
ser-AT-oh-SORE-us

*Ceratosaurus*'s name means "horned lizard" and refers to the rounded horn above its nostrils. It also had a horn in front of each eye. A row of low spines ran down its neck, back, and tail—an uncommon feature for a theropod.

**DATE** 150–144 mya (Late Jurassic)

**SIZE** 20 ft (6 m) long

**FOSSIL LOCATIONS**
United States and Portugal

**HABITAT** Forests

**DIET** Dinosaurs and other reptiles

# Liliensternus
LIL-ee-en-STERN-us

In its time, *Liliensternus* was the largest predator on land. Its long hind legs allowed it to run fast after its prosauropod prey. This theropod probably stalked its victims before attacking.

**DATE** 210 mya (Late Triassic)

**SIZE** 16½–20 ft (5–6 m) long

**FOSSIL LOCATION** Germany

**HABITAT** Forests

**DIET** Dinosaurs

## Dilophosaurus
di-LOAF-oh-SORE-us

This animal is best-known for the two parallel, platelike crests on its snout. Scientists believe these were used in a display for attracting mates.

**DATE** 201–189 mya (Early Jurassic)

**SIZE** 20 ft (6 m) long

**FOSSIL LOCATION** US

**HABITAT** Riverbanks

**DIET** Small animals and fish

## Monolophosaurus
mono-LOAF-oh-SORE-us

With a thick crest on its head, *Monolophosaurus* had one of the biggest and oddest of skulls. The hollow crest may have helped to produce noises that warned off rivals.

**DATE** 180–159 mya (Middle Jurassic)

**SIZE** 20 ft (6 m) long

**FOSSIL LOCATION** China

**HABITAT** Forests

**DIET** Dinosaurs

# Cryolophosaurus
CRY-oh-LOAF-oh-SORE-us

The largest known theropod from the Early Jurassic, *Cryolophosaurus* had slender arms and long legs. It was also the first theropod to be discovered in Antarctica. The crest on its head was unusual in shape, curving upward and forward over the skull.

**DATE** 190–185 mya (Early Jurassic)

**SIZE** 21½ ft (6.5 m) long

**FOSSIL LOCATION** Antarctica

**HABITAT** Open plains

**DIET** Dinosaurs

People nicknamed this dinosaur Elvisaurus because its head crest reminded them of Elvis Presley's hair.

# Baryonyx
## bah-ree-ON-ix

A fish-eating theropod, *Baryonyx* had an unusual curved claw on its thumb or index finger. It used the claws as hooks to kill its prey, much like bears do today.

**DATE** 125 mya (Early Cretaceous)

**SIZE** 29½ ft (9 m) long

**FOSSIL LOCATIONS** British Isles, Spain, and Portugal

**HABITAT** Riverbanks

**DIET** Fish and dinosaurs

# Suchomimus
## soo-ko-MIME-us

A close relative of *Baryonyx*, this predator had a long, crocodilelike snout and a slim jaw with more than 100 teeth that pointed backward. *Suchomimus* used its teeth and long arms to hold slippery prey.

Teeth at tip of snout were longer than those at the back

Crocodilelike jaw

**DATE** 112 mya (Early Cretaceous)

**SIZE** 29½ ft (9 m) long

**FOSSIL LOCATION** Africa

**HABITAT** Mangrove swamps

**DIET** Fish and possibly other animals

# Spinosaurus
SPINE-oh-SORE-us

*Spinosaurus* is one of the longest theropods known. It had a sail-like structure running down its back, supported by spines made of bone. This gave it the name *Spinosaurus*, meaning "spine lizard." Scientists believe that this predator may have used its sail to control its body temperature.

| | |
|---|---|
| **DATE** | 97 mya (Late Cretaceous) |
| **SIZE** | 59 ft (18 m) long |
| **FOSSIL LOCATIONS** | Morocco, Libya, and Egypt |
| **HABITAT** | Tropical swamps |
| **DIET** | Fish and dinosaurs |

Sail supported by spines

Large, conical teeth

Raised on bones 6½ ft (2 m) long, the sail of *Spinosaurus* was an impressive sight.

# Allosaurus
al-oh-SORE-us

This fierce predator had a massive skull, powerful jaws, and a long tail. Sturdy bones supported its jaw and bladelike teeth. The skull enabled *Allosaurus* to chop flesh rapidly, unlike the slow, bone-crushing skull of *Tyrannosaurus*.

**DATE** 150 mya (Late Jurassic)

**SIZE** 39 ft (12 m) long

**FOSSIL LOCATIONS**
US and Portugal

**HABITAT** Open plains

**DIET** Large plant-eating dinosaurs

## Carcharodontosaurus
CAR-ka-roe-DON-toe-SORE-us

Twice the weight of an elephant, this enormous theropod used its massive jaws equipped with sawlike teeth to kill prey. The scientists who first discovered it found its teeth similar to those of the great white shark, *Carcharodon,* and named it *Carcharodontosaurus.*

**DATE** 100 mya (Early Cretaceous)

**SIZE** 46 ft (14 m) long

**FOSSIL LOCATIONS** Morocco, Tunisia, and Egypt

**HABITAT** Floodplains and mangroves

**DIET** Large plant-eating dinosaurs

## Giganotosaurus
GEEG-ah-NOTE-ih-SORE-us

Similar in size to *Tyrannosaurus*, *Giganotosaurus* was as heavy as 125 people. Despite its size, it could probably run at 30 mph (50 kph) when chasing its prey.

**DATE** 112–90 mya (Early Cretaceous)

**SIZE** 43 ft (13 m) long

**FOSSIL LOCATION** Argentina

**HABITAT** Warm swamps

**DIET** Large dinosaurs

## Sinraptor
SIN-rap-ter

A close relative of *Allosaurus*, *Sinraptor* was a formidable hunter. Tooth marks on a skull suggest that it might have fought with its own kind.

**DATE** 169–142 mya (Middle–Late Jurassic)

**SIZE** 24½ ft (7.5 m) long

**FOSSIL LOCATION** China

**HABITAT** Forests

**DIET** Large plant-eating dinosaurs

# Powerful jaws lined with
# bone-crunching
## blades made *Tarbosaurus* the most fearsome predator on the plains of China

**TARBOSAURUS**
*Tarbosaurus* was a close relative of *Tyrannosaurus*, and both of them belong to a family of theropods called tyrannosaurids. *Tarbosaurus* preyed on smaller dinosaurs, such as *Barsboldia*, which was a hadrosaur.

## Albertosaurus
al-BERT-oh-SORE-us

This lightly built predator had slender hind limbs and small forelimbs and may have been a swift runner. Some scientists believe that *Albertosaurus* lived and hunted in packs.

| | |
|---|---|
| **DATE** | 75 mya (Late Cretaceous) |
| **SIZE** | 29½ ft (9 m) long |
| **FOSSIL LOCATION** | Canada |
| **HABITAT** | Forests |
| **DIET** | Dinosaurs |

## Compsognathus
COMP-sog-NAITH-us

Running on the tips of its toes, this chicken-sized predator could easily outpace fast-moving prey. Its long tail helped in balancing and making sharp turns while running.

| | |
|---|---|
| **DATE** | 150 mya (Late Jurassic) |
| **SIZE** | 4¼ ft (1.3 m) long |
| **FOSSIL LOCATIONS** | Germany and France |
| **HABITAT** | Scrublands and marshes |
| **DIET** | Lizards, mammals, and small dinosaurs |

## Tyrannosaurus
TIE-ran-oh-SORE-us

*Tyrannosaurus* was as long as a bus and twice as heavy as an elephant. This fearsome predator had pointed teeth that could tear skin and muscle, and even crush bone. Three-toed feet allowed this heavy animal to plod along at a steady trot. Its tiny arms, with two claws on each, were probably used to hold the prey during feeding.

| | |
|---|---|
| **DATE** | 70–65 mya (Late Cretaceous) |
| **SIZE** | 39 ft (12 m) long |
| **FOSSIL LOCATION** | North America |
| **HABITAT** | Forests and swamps |
| **DIET** | Large dinosaurs |

Although shown in the film *Jurassic Park*, *Tyrannosaurus* actually lived in the Cretaceous Period.

## Guanlong
GWON-long

*Guanlong* means "crowned dragon," the name reflecting the striking crest on the theropod's head. It was a close relative of early feathered dinosaurs and had a coat of fuzzy feathers itself.

**DATE** 160 mya (Late Jurassic)

**SIZE** 8¼ ft (2.5 m) long

**FOSSIL LOCATION** China

**HABITAT** Forests

**DIET** Dinosaurs and other animals

## Proceratosaurus
PRO-seh-RAT-oh-SORE-us

The only fossil of this crested dinosaur is this skull found in 1910. It is thought to be a small dinosaur and a close relative of *Guanlong*.

**DATE** 175 mya (Middle Jurassic)

**SIZE** 6½ ft (2 m) long

**FOSSIL LOCATION** British Isles

**HABITAT** Forests

**DIET** Dinosaurs and other animals

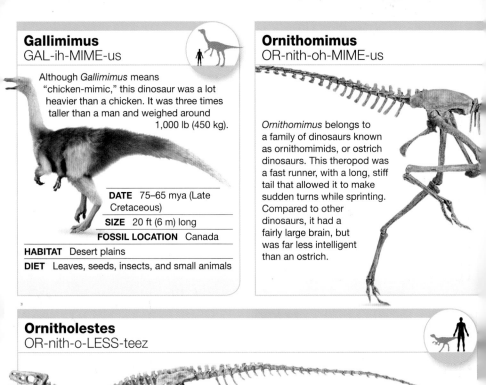

## Gallimimus
GAL-ih-MIME-us

Although *Gallimimus* means "chicken-mimic," this dinosaur was a lot heavier than a chicken. It was three times taller than a man and weighed around 1,000 lb (450 kg).

| | |
|---|---|
| **DATE** | 75–65 mya (Late Cretaceous) |
| **SIZE** | 20 ft (6 m) long |
| **FOSSIL LOCATION** | Canada |
| **HABITAT** | Desert plains |
| **DIET** | Leaves, seeds, insects, and small animals |

## Ornithomimus
OR-nith-oh-MIME-us

*Ornithomimus* belongs to a family of dinosaurs known as ornithomimids, or ostrich dinosaurs. This theropod was a fast runner, with a long, stiff tail that allowed it to make sudden turns while sprinting. Compared to other dinosaurs, it had a fairly large brain, but was far less intelligent than an ostrich.

## Ornitholestes
OR-nith-o-LESS-teez

A small and lightly built body made *Ornitholestes* a swift and efficient predator. It had long front teeth with flattened tips that helped it catch prey.

| | |
|---|---|
| **DATE** | 156–145 mya (Late Jurassic) |
| **SIZE** | 6½ ft (2 m) long |
| **FOSSIL LOCATION** | United States |
| **HABITAT** | Forests |
| **DIET** | Small animals, such as insects, lizards, and frogs |

*Long, powerful grasping fingers*

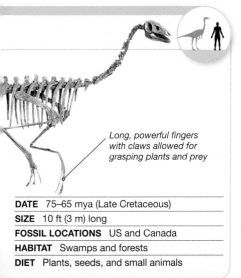

*Long, powerful fingers with claws allowed for grasping plants and prey*

**DATE** 75–65 mya (Late Cretaceous)

**SIZE** 10 ft (3 m) long

**FOSSIL LOCATIONS** US and Canada

**HABITAT** Swamps and forests

**DIET** Plants, seeds, and small animals

# Caudipteryx
caw-DIP-ter-ix

Although its body was covered in feathers, *Caudipteryx* was unable to fly. Scientists believe it used its feathers for display and to keep itself warm.

**DATE** 130–120 mya (Early Cretaceous)

**SIZE** 3¼ ft (1 m) long

**FOSSIL LOCATION** China

**HABITAT** Lake sides and riverbeds

**DIET** Plants, seeds, and small animals

# Citipati
SIH-tee-PAH-tee

*Citipati* had a distinctive crest on its head that was made of horny keratin. In addition to plants, this theropod probably also fed on eggs and baby dinosaurs, ripping them apart with its beak, just as eagles do today.

**DATE** 75 mya (Late Cretaceous)

**SIZE** 10 ft (3 m) long

**FOSSIL LOCATION** Mongolia

**HABITAT** Open plains

**DIET** Plants and animals

*Troodon* had the largest brain of all dinosaurs, relative to its body size.

## Microraptor
my-CROW-rap-ter

One of the smallest dinosaurs, *Microraptor* had long, birdlike feathers on its arms and legs. However, unlike birds, which flap their feathered wings and fly, the wings of *Microraptor* were not big enough to support the animal's weight and so it could only glide from branch to branch. It probably did so to search for prey and to escape predators.

| | |
|---|---|
| **DATE** | 130–125 mya (Early Cretaceous) |
| **SIZE** | 3¼ ft (1 m) long |
| **FOSSIL LOCATION** | China |
| **HABITAT** | Forests |
| **DIET** | Small mammals, lizards, and insects |

## Troodon
TROH-o-don

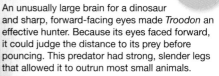

An unusually large brain for a dinosaur and sharp, forward-facing eyes made *Troodon* an effective hunter. Because its eyes faced forward, it could judge the distance to its prey before pouncing. This predator had strong, slender legs that allowed it to outrun most small animals.

| | |
|---|---|
| **DATE** | 74–65 mya (Late Cretaceous) |
| **SIZE** | 10 ft (3 m) long |
| **FOSSIL LOCATION** | North America |
| **HABITAT** | Forests |
| **DIET** | Small animals and possibly plants |

## Velociraptor
vel-OSS-a-rap-ter

About the size of a wolf, this theropod used its long clawed arms to grapple and bring down prey. It is one of the best-known of all dinosaurs, having been shown in films such as *Jurassic Park*.

| | |
|---|---|
| **DATE** | 85 mya (Late Cretaceous) |
| **SIZE** | 6½ ft (2 m) long |
| **FOSSIL LOCATION** | Mongolia |
| **HABITAT** | Scrublands and deserts |
| **DIET** | Lizards, mammals, and small dinosaurs |

## Deinonychus
dye-NON-ee-cuss

Famous for its large toe claws, *Deinonychus* was a fierce predator. Some experts think that the sickle-shaped claws may have been used to slash the throat or belly of prey.

| | |
|---|---|
| **DATE** | 115–108 mya (Early Cretaceous) |
| **SIZE** | 10 ft (3 m) long |
| **FOSSIL LOCATION** | US |
| **HABITAT** | Swamps and forests |
| **DIET** | Small dinosaurs |

Many *Citipati* fossils have been found crouching over eggs in nests, seeming to brood the eggs **just like a bird**

### CITIPATI

*Citipati* belongs to a family of theropods called oviraptorosaurs. These dinosaurs had parrotlike beaks and their bodies were covered with feathers. *Caudipteryx* and *Oviraptor* were also members of this family.

# Early birds

Birds began as small, feathered, toothed dinosaurs with long, bony tails and small flight muscles. Over time, they evolved shorter tails, stronger muscles, and a lighter skeleton.

FOCUS ON...
## FEATURES
Early birds had many features that are absent in their modern cousins.

## Archaeopteryx
ar-kee-OP-ter-ix

*Archaeopteryx* was capable of weakly powered flight. Weak flight muscles and a bony tail meant that it was a clumsy flier. It was long considered the earliest bird. Some scientists now think that a theropod called *Xiaotingia* may have been more closely related to early birds.

**DATE**  150 mya (Late Jurassic)

**SIZE**  12 in (30 cm) long

**FOSSIL LOCATION**  Germany

**HABITAT**  Forests and lakes

**DIET**  Insects and reptiles

▲ The fingers on the forelimbs had claws, which helped the early birds to climb.

▲ The tails of early birds were long and reptilelike, unlike the bony stump of modern birds.

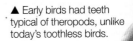

▲ Early birds had teeth typical of theropods, unlike today's toothless birds.

# Ichthyornis
## ICK-thee-OR-niss

Like modern birds, this gull-sized seabird had a deep keelbone—an extension of the breastbone—that anchored its flight muscles. It also had a boxlike rib structure similar to modern birds. It was still a primitive bird, however, and had small, sharp teeth.

Long beak with sharp teeth

Clawed feet

**DATE**  90–75 mya (Late Cretaceous)

**SIZE**  23½ in (60 cm) long

**FOSSIL LOCATION**  United States

**HABITAT**  Seashores

**DIET**  Fish

# Vegavis
## VAY-gah-viss

*Vegavis* is distantly related to today's ducks and geese. The discovery of *Vegavis* shows that some of today's bird families had already evolved in the Cretaceous Period.

**DATE**  65 mya (Late Cretaceous)

**SIZE**  23½ in (60 cm) long

**FOSSIL LOCATION**  Antarctica

**HABITAT**  Seashores

**DIET**  Water plants

Webbed feet

## FOCUS ON...
### FEATURES
Some characteristics were common to all prosauropods.

▲ Prosauropods had a massive, clawed thumb used to rake in plants.

▲ Prosauropods had a high snout and long, slender jaws.

▲ Small, leaf-shaped teeth could easily slice through tough stems.

# Prosauropods

These early plant-eating relatives of sauropods evolved from small meat-eating dinosaurs in the Triassic. Over time, they grew taller and heavier, with long necks and strong hind legs that let them reach high tree branches. They had hands with fingers and thumbs.

### Efraasia
e-FRAHS-ee-a

*Efraasia* had a small head with a long neck. Its five-fingered hands had a large thumb claw. It may have walked on all fours to browse on leaves, but probably ran on its hind legs.

| | |
|---|---|
| **DATE** | 210 mya (Late Triassic) |
| **SIZE** | 20–23 ft (6–7 m) long |
| **FOSSIL LOCATION** | Germany |
| **HABITAT** | Dry plains |
| **DIET** | Plants and possibly animals |

# Thecodontosaurus
THEE-co-DON-toe-SORE-us

The unusual leaf-shaped, sawlike teeth of this prosauropod resembled those of a modern-day monitor lizard, but were attached to distinct sockets in its jaws. This inspired the name *Thecodontosaurus*, which means "socket-toothed lizard."

| | |
|---|---|
| **DATE** | 225–208 mya (Late Triassic) |
| **SIZE** | 6½ ft (2 m) long |
| **FOSSIL LOCATION** | British Isles |
| **HABITAT** | Island forests |
| **DIET** | Plants and possibly animals |

Long neck

Short forelimb

# Anchisaurus
ankee-SORE-us

This early cousin of the sauropods had a shallow skull and a flexible spine. It had a narrow snout and pointed teeth in its upper jaw. *Anchisaurus* was probably an omnivore, feeding on small reptiles along with leaves.

| | |
|---|---|
| **DATE** | 190 mya (Early Jurassic) |
| **SIZE** | 6½ ft (2 m) long |
| **FOSSIL LOCATION** | United States |
| **HABITAT** | Forests |
| **DIET** | Leaves and small reptiles |

Clawed toe

# Plateosaurus
PLATE-ee-oh-SORE-us

One of the best-known prosauropods, *Plateosaurus* could probably stand upright like a kangaroo, rearing on its hind limbs and stretching its legs to eat leaves from trees. Its sharp teeth could easily slice through tough leaf stems.

**DATE** 220–210 mya (Late Triassic)

**SIZE** 26 ft (8 m) long

**FOSSIL LOCATIONS** Germany, Switzerland, Norway, and Greenland

**HABITAT** Open plains

**DIET** Plants

## Lufengosaurus
loo-FENG-oh-SORE-us

This prosauropod had a massive claw on each of its thumbs that probably helped to grasp tree branches while feeding. *Lufengosaurus* used its widely spaced, bladelike teeth to rake leaves off branches.

**DATE** 200–180 mya (Early Jurassic)

**SIZE** 16½ ft (5 m) long

**FOSSIL LOCATION** China

**HABITAT** Forests

**DIET** Plants, including cycad and conifer leaves

## Massospondylus
MASS-oh-SPON-dill-us

Fossils of *Massospondylus* show that it had a bulky body with a long tail. Five-fingered hands with massive thumb claws may have been used to tear off branches and stems. It may also have used its small, coarse teeth to chew on meat.

**DATE** 200–183 mya (Early Jurassic)

**SIZE** 13–20 ft (4–6 m) long

**FOSSIL LOCATION** South Africa

**HABITAT** Forests

**DIET** Plants and animals

# Sauropods

The largest creatures ever to walk on the Earth, these lumbering giants had long necks and tails and pillarlike legs, but relatively small heads. They lived in herds and walked on all fours.

FOCUS ON...
## FOOTPRINTS
Sauropod footprints have been found across the world.

## Diplodocus
dip-LOD-oh-kuss

Probably one of the longest dinosaurs ever, *Diplodocus* had a tail that was as long as the rest of its body. Some scientists think that it raised its neck to browse on treetops, while others believe that it swung its head from side to side, feeding on shrubs.

| | |
|---|---|
| **DATE** | 150–145 mya (Late Jurassic) |
| **SIZE** | 98½–110 ft (30–33.5 m) long |
| **FOSSIL LOCATION** | United States |
| **HABITAT** | Plains |
| **DIET** | Plants |

Tail bones become narrow at the tip

*Diplodocus* could move its tail at very high speed, producing a whiplike crack, which may have frightened off predators.

◀ In 1997, paleontologists discovered sauropod footprints in fossilized mud in a beach near Broome in Australia.

◀ The Purgatoire River track site in Colorado has more than 100 dinosaur trackways. Sauropod footprints can be seen here.

# Apatosaurus
a-PAT-oh-SORE-us

Also known as *Brontosaurus*, this plant-eating giant was probably shorter than other sauropods and had thicker legs. *Apatosaurus* may have knocked down trees in search of food, much like elephants do today.

| | |
|---|---|
| **DATE** | 150 mya (Late Jurassic) |
| **SIZE** | 75½ ft (23 m) long |
| **FOSSIL LOCATION** | United States |
| **HABITAT** | Forests |
| **DIET** | Plants |

Long, complex neck bones provide framework for supporting the head

A fully grown *Apatosaurus* could weigh as much as four elephants.

## Barosaurus
BAH-roe-SORE-us

With a neck as long as 31 ft (9.5 m), this sauropod had an advantage over other dinosaurs when it came to reaching leaves right at the tops of trees. Its teeth were shaped like pegs, allowing it to rake leaves easily off the branches.

**DATE**  155–145 mya (Late Jurassic)

**SIZE**  92 ft (28 m) long

**FOSSIL LOCATION**  United States

**HABITAT**  Forests and plains

**DIET**  Plants

Like today's cows, *Barosaurus* may have carried bacteria in its intestines that digested its food.

## Amargasaurus
ah-MAR-gah-SORE-us

A double row of spines ran down *Amargasaurus*'s neck, ending at its tail. There may have been a web of skin between the rows, forming a sail used for display.

**DATE**  130 mya (Early Cretaceous)

**SIZE**  36 ft (11 m) long

**FOSSIL LOCATION**  Argentina

**HABITAT**  Forests

**DIET**  Plants

## Dicraeosaurus
DIE-cray-oh-SORE-us

The bony spines running down the neck and back of *Dicraeosaurus* formed a ridgelike structure. It may have used the ridge for display, defense, or for controlling body temperature.

| | |
|---|---|
| **DATE** | 150 mya (Late Jurassic) |
| **SIZE** | 39 ft (12 m) long |
| **FOSSIL LOCATION** | Tanzania |
| **HABITAT** | Forests |
| **DIET** | Plants |

## Vulcanodon
vul-KAN-o-don

This sauropod was named *Vulcanodon*, since its first fossils were found in rocks near volcanoes. Like other sauropods, it had short, elephantlike feet that were not suitable for running.

| | |
|---|---|
| **DATE** | 208–201 mya (Late Triassic) |
| **SIZE** | 23 ft (7 m) long |
| **FOSSIL LOCATION** | Zimbabwe |
| **HABITAT** | Forests and plains |
| **DIET** | Plants |

**Barosaurus** could browse the treetops 49 ft (15 m) above the ground—the height of a **four-story building**

**BAROSAURUS**
A relative of the sauropod *Diplodocus*, *Barosaurus* had a very long neck. It had 15 cervical vertebrae (neck bones), some of which were more than 3¼ ft (1 m) long. This sauropod lived in herds, moving through the Jurassic forests in search of food.

# Titanosaurus
tie-TAN-oh-SORE-us

*Scientists believe that this dinosaur had bony studs on its back, much like its relative* Saltasaurus

*Titanosaurus* is known only from fossil remains of limb bones. Many scientists believe that it had a typical sauropod body shape with a small head, short neck, and bulky body. Others, however, argue that the fossils belong to other dinosaurs, and *Titanosaurus* is not a separate species at all.

| | |
|---|---|
| **DATE** | 80–65 mya (Late Cretaceous) |
| **SIZE** | 39–59 ft (12–18 m) long |
| **FOSSIL LOCATIONS** | Asia, Europe, and Africa |
| **HABITAT** | Forests and plains |
| **DIET** | Plants |

# Saltasaurus
SALT-ah-SORE-us

Although smaller than many other sauropods, *Saltasaurus* had bony plates and studs running down its back, which defended it from large predators. Its neck was shorter than that of most sauropods and, unlike most of them, this animal lacked claws on its front feet.

| | |
|---|---|
| **DATE** | 80–65 mya (Late Cretaceous) |
| **SIZE** | 39 ft (12 m) long |
| **FOSSIL LOCATION** | Argentina |
| **HABITAT** | Forests and open plains |
| **DIET** | Plants |

# Argentinosaurus
ARE-jen-teen-oh-SORE-us

*Argentinosaurus* was one of the largest and heaviest land animals ever to walk on the Earth. It was longer than a tennis court and 20 times heavier than an elephant.

**DATE**   112–95 mya (Early Cretaceous)

**SIZE**   108–134 ft (33–41 m) long

**FOSSIL LOCATION**   Argentina

**HABITAT**   Forests and open plains

**DIET**   Conifers

# Mamenchisaurus
ma-MEN-chee-SORE-us

*Mamenchisaurus* had one of the longest necks of any known animal. The 19 long bones allowed it to move the neck freely and reach for food with great ease. It had a small, pointed head. It was named after a Chinese village, where its fossils were first found.

**DATE** 155–145 mya (Late Jurassic)

**SIZE** 85 ft (26 m) long

**FOSSIL LOCATION** China

**HABITAT** Riverbanks, forests, and open plains

**DIET** Trees and other plants

# Brachiosaurus
BRACK-ee-oh-SORE-us

This sauropod used its long neck to feed on treetop leaves at heights greater than 49 ft (15 m), which is twice as high as any giraffe can reach. *Brachiosaurus* used its spoonlike teeth to snip off and eat an amazing 441 lb (200 kg) of leaves per day.

**DATE** 150–145 mya (Late Jurassic)

**SIZE** 75½ ft (23 m) long

**FOSSIL LOCATION** United States

**HABITAT** Forests and plains

**DIET** Leaves and twigs of conifers

*Brachiosaurus* weighed as much as 12 African elephants—an incredible 30–50 tons.

## Camarasaurus
KAM-a-ra-SORE-us

*Camarasaurus* means "chambered lizard." The dinosaur got this name because of the large air spaces inside some of the hollow bones connected to its lungs. These chambers helped reduce the animal's body weight.

| | |
|---|---|
| **DATE** | 150–140 mya (Late Jurassic) |
| **SIZE** | 59 ft (18 m) long |
| **FOSSIL LOCATION** | United States |
| **HABITAT** | Open plains |
| **DIET** | Tree leaves |

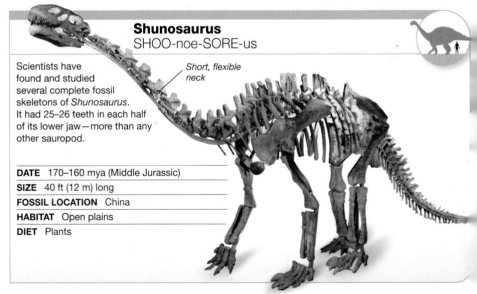

## Shunosaurus
SHOO-noe-SORE-us

Scientists have found and studied several complete fossil skeletons of *Shunosaurus*. It had 25–26 teeth in each half of its lower jaw—more than any other sauropod.

*Short, flexible neck*

| | |
|---|---|
| **DATE** | 170–160 mya (Middle Jurassic) |
| **SIZE** | 40 ft (12 m) long |
| **FOSSIL LOCATION** | China |
| **HABITAT** | Open plains |
| **DIET** | Plants |

# Nemegtosaurus
nem-EGG-toe-SORE-us

A close relative of *Saltasaurus*, this sauropod is known only from a single fossil skull found in the 1970s. *Nemegtosaurus* was named after the Nemegt Basin in the Gobi Desert of Mongolia.

| | |
|---|---|
| **DATE** | 80–65 mya (Late Cretaceous) |
| **SIZE** | 49 ft (15 m) long |
| **FOSSIL LOCATION** | Mongolia |
| **HABITAT** | Forests |
| **DIET** | Plants |

# Stegosaurs and relatives

Many dinosaurs evolved structures on their skin that helped them in defense against the predatory theropods. The stegosaurs, with rows of plates and spines along their backs, must have made a spectacular sight in the Jurassic forests.

▲ The plates on the back were probably used in courtship displays or perhaps to regulate body temperature by radiating heat away from the body.

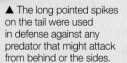

▲ The long pointed spikes on the tail were used in defense against any predator that might attack from behind or the sides.

### Scutellosaurus
SKOO-tell-oh-SORE-us

A relative of the stegosaurs, *Scutellosaurus* was an early ornithischian. This lightweight creature had hundreds of small bony scutes, or studs, on its skin.

| | |
|---|---|
| **DATE** | 196 mya (Early Jurassic) |
| **SIZE** | 3¼ ft (1 m) long |
| **FOSSIL LOCATION** | United States |
| **HABITAT** | Forests |
| **DIET** | Plants |

# Stegosaurus
## STEG-oh-SORE-us

This animal was the largest of all the stegosaurs. It featured an alternating double row of flat, diamond-shaped plates running along its arched back. The plates were attached to the skin and were probably covered by keratin, the substance that forms horns and fingernails. *Stegosaurus*'s forelimbs were shorter than its hind limbs, so it walked with its hips higher than its shoulders. Its spine bones were tall and gave the animal a high, arched shape.

**DATE** 150–145 mya (Late Jurassic)

**SIZE** 29½ ft (9 m)

**FOSSIL LOCATIONS** US and Portugal

**HABITAT** Forests

**DIET** Plants

This dinosaur was named *Stegosaurus*, meaning "roof lizard," because its discoverer thought the plates on its back looked like roof tiles.

A predator would have broken
its teeth on the rows of
# bony studs
# and spikes
running from *Scelidosaurus*'s
head to its tail

**SCELIDOSAURUS**
*Scelidosaurus* lived in the Early Jurassic and belonged to the same group of ancestral armored dinosaurs as *Scutellosaurus* (see p. 72). Its bony armor was covered in keratin—the material that forms nails and horns.

More than 900 *Kentrosaurus* bones were found in a single fossil site in Tanzania.

## Huayangosaurus
HWAH-YANG-oh-SORE-us

Most stegosaurs have long hind limbs and short forelimbs, but all four of *Huayangosaurus*'s limbs were the same length. It was also different from later species as it had a shorter, broader snout, with teeth on the front of its upper jaw.

| | |
|---|---|
| **DATE** | 165 mya (Middle Jurassic) |
| **SIZE** | 13 ft (4 m) long |
| **FOSSIL LOCATION** | China |
| **HABITAT** | River valleys |
| **DIET** | Ferns, leaves, and cycad fruit |

# Kentrosaurus
KEN-troh-SORE-us

Seven pairs of bony plates lined the neck and back of this herbivore and may have been used for display. When attacked by a predator, *Kentrosaurus* probably lashed out its tail, using the long tail spikes to injure the attacker.

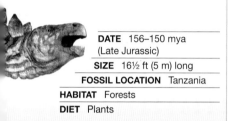

| | |
|---|---|
| **DATE** | 156–150 mya (Late Jurassic) |
| **SIZE** | 16½ ft (5 m) long |
| **FOSSIL LOCATION** | Tanzania |
| **HABITAT** | Forests |
| **DIET** | Plants |

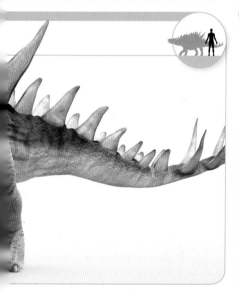

# Tuojiangosaurus
TOO-YANG-oh-SORE-us

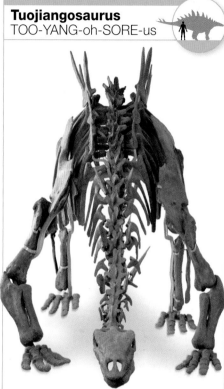

A close relative of *Stegosaurus*, *Tuojiangosaurus* had a long, shallow snout, beaklike jaws, and spikes on its tail. It shared these features with other stegosaurs.

| | |
|---|---|
| **DATE** | 160–150 mya (Late Jurassic) |
| **SIZE** | 23 ft (7 m) long |
| **FOSSIL LOCATION** | China |
| **HABITAT** | Forests |
| **DIET** | Plants |

# Nodosaurs

A family of armored dinosaurs called the nodosaurs appeared in the Jurassic Period. Their armor was made of rows of bony deposits that formed plates and spikes on their skin. The armor helped mainly in defense but it also became important in display and combat between rivals.

## Gastonia
gas-TOE-nee-ah

This low-slung and heavy nodosaur had thick, bony scutes on its back and tail, many of which were extended into bladelike spikes. If attacked, *Gastonia* could severely injure a predator with its spiked tail. The top of its skull was extra thick, suggesting that males may have had head-butting contests over territory.

| | |
|---|---|
| **DATE** | 125 mya (Early Cretaceous) |
| **SIZE** | 13 ft (4 m) long |
| **FOSSIL LOCATION** | United States |
| **HABITAT** | Forests |
| **DIET** | Plants |

## Edmontonia
ED-mon-TOE-nee-a

*Edmontonia* would probably scare off predators by charging and lunging at them with its spearlike shoulder spikes. It may have also used its spikes to fight with others of its kind over territory or mates.

| | |
|---|---|
| **DATE** | 75–65 mya (Late Cretaceous) |
| **SIZE** | 23 ft (7 m) long |
| **FOSSIL LOCATION** | North America |
| **HABITAT** | Forests |
| **DIET** | Low-growing plants |

## Sauropelta
SORE-oh-PELT-ah

This dinosaur's enormous neck spines helped to protect the animal against predators such as *Deinonychus* (see p. 51). A thick shield of armor plates covered this nodosaur's back and tail, giving it the name *Sauropelta*, which means "shield lizard."

**DATE** 120–110 mya (Early Cretaceous)

**SIZE** 16½ ft (5 m) long

**FOSSIL LOCATION** United States

**HABITAT** Forests

**DIET** Plants

## Gargoyleosaurus
GAR-goil-oh-SORE-us

Unlike most other armored dinosaurs, *Gargoyleosaurus* had seven conical teeth at the front of its upper jaw. These may have made it easier for the animal to tear off leaves and stems from plants. Armor plates lined the nodosaur's back, while triangular horns projected from its head and cheeks.

**DATE** 155–145 mya (Late Jurassic)

**SIZE** 13 ft (4 m) long

**FOSSIL LOCATION** US

**HABITAT** Forests

**DIET** Low-growing plants

# Ankylosaurs

This family of armored dinosaurs evolved in the Cretaceous Period. Unlike nodosaurs, ankylosaurs had broad, triangular heavily armored heads and lacked long spines on the sides of their body. Their tails often ended in bony clubs. The hefty clubs of some ankylosaurs may have been heavy enough to cripple predators.

## Ankylosaurus
ANK-ill-oh-SORE-us

The largest of all ankylosaurs, *Ankylosaurus* was covered from head to tail with bony plates. Even its eyelids had small plates covering them. Plates at the end of the tail were fused together, forming a sledgehammerlike club, which could be swung at theropods with bone-shattering force.

| | |
|---|---|
| **DATE** | 70–65 mya (Late Cretaceous) |
| **SIZE** | 20 ft (6 m) long |
| **FOSSIL LOCATION** | North America |
| **HABITAT** | Forests |
| **DIET** | Plants |

Bony plate on upper body

Bony club at end of tail

# Minmi
MIN-mee

One of the smallest ankylosaurs, *Minmi* had extra bones along its back that may have supported its back muscles. It had small, leaf-shaped teeth and a sharp beak.

**DATE**
120–115 mya
(Early Cretaceous)

**SIZE**  10 ft (3 m) long

**FOSSIL LOCATION**  Australia

**HABITAT**  Forests and open plains

**DIET**  Leaves, seeds, and fruit

# Euoplocephalus
YOU-owe-plo-SEFF-ah-luss

*Euoplocephalus* was a massive, club-tailed ankylosaur. Although a heavy animal, it had powerful legs that made it nimble on its feet. Its armor, speed, and tail club provided it with a triple defense against predators.

**DATE**  70–65 mya (Late Cretaceous)

**SIZE**  20 ft (6 m) long

**FOSSIL LOCATION**  North America

**HABITAT**  Forests

**DIET**  Plants

# Any predator that got past the
## sledgehammer tail
of *Euoplocephalus* would be
stopped by the spikes that
covered its neck and back

### *EUOPLOCEPHALUS*
In Late Cretaceous North America, *Euoplocephalus*
had to fend off attacks from giant predators, such
as the theropod *Gorgosaurus*. The ankylosaur's
tailbones were fused together into a club, which
could deliver crippling injuries to an aggressor.

## FOCUS ON...
### DIVERSITY
The ornithopods diversified into many different types of dinosaur.

# Ornithopods

The ornithischians were plant-eaters with short beaks. The ornithopods made up one group of ornithischians. Some had chewing teeth that pulped plant matter. Many moved in big herds and on two legs, while some of the bigger ones usually walked on all fours.

▲ Hypsilophodonts were small, two-legged plant-eaters that could run very fast.

▲ Iguanodonts had horselike faces and ranged in size from small dinosaurs to giants.

▲ Hadrosaurs had beaks like ducks and are known as "duck-billed" dinosaurs.

## Heterodontosaurus
### HET-er-oh-DON-toe-SORE-us

*Heterodontosaurus* was a typical plant-eating ornithischian, except that it had three types of teeth—sharp front teeth that helped to snip off leaves, closely packed chewing teeth at the back of its mouth, and pointed, fanglike teeth, which it probably used in defense.

**DATE** 200–190 mya (Early Jurassic)

**SIZE** 3¼ ft (1 m) long

**FOSSIL LOCATION** South Africa

**HABITAT** Scrubland

**DIET** Plants, tubers, and possibly insects

*Horny beak helped to snip off leaves*

## Lesothosaurus
li-SUE-too-SORE-us

This turkey-sized ornithopod was agile and could probably easily escape predators. It had big eyes on the sides of its head that gave it a good all-around view of approaching threats.

**DATE** 200–190 mya
(Early Jurassic)

**SIZE** 3¼ ft (1 m) long

**FOSSIL LOCATION**
South Africa

**HABITAT** Deserts

**DIET** Leaves and perhaps dead animals and insects

## Dryosaurus
DRY-oh-SORE-us

*Dryosaurus* is the best-known member of a group of small ornithopods called dryosaurids. It could run fast and it may have flicked its tail sideways to make sharp turns for dodging obstacles or escaping predators.

**DATE** 155–145 mya (Late Jurassic)

**SIZE** 10 ft (3 m) long

**FOSSIL LOCATION** United States

**HABITAT** Forests

**DIET** Leaves and shoots

## Leaellynasaura
lee-ELL-in-ah-SORE-ah

*Leaellynasaura* lived in Australia, which was much closer to the South Pole in the Cretaceous Period than it is today. This small ornithopod faced long winters, going without sunlight for many months.

**DATE**
105 mya
(Early Cretaceous)

**SIZE** 6½ ft (2 m) long

**FOSSIL LOCATION**
Australia

**HABITAT** Forests

**DIET** Plants

## Tenontosaurus
ten-NON-toe-SORE-us

*Tenontosaurus* had a narrow but deep skull and a rather stiff and bony tail. This animal was probably often hunted by packs of small theropods called *Deinonychus*. Teeth of this predator have been found along with *Tenontosaurus*'s bones, suggesting that the ornithopod may have put up a fight before being brought down.

**DATE** 115–108 mya (Early Cretaceous)

**SIZE** 23 ft (7 m) long

**FOSSIL LOCATION** US

**HABITAT** Forests

**DIET** Plants

## Hypsilophodon
HIP-sih-LOAF-oh-don

Fossil footprints of *Hypsilophodon* suggest that it lived and moved in herds, much like deer do today. Its long legs and feet and stiff tail made it a fast-running animal, able to escape predators running only on its hind legs and balancing with its tail.

*Five-fingered hand*

*Long, slender foot*

**DATE** 125–120 mya (Early Cretaceous)

**SIZE** 6½ ft (2 m) long

**FOSSIL LOCATIONS** England and Spain

**HABITAT** Forests

**DIET** Plants

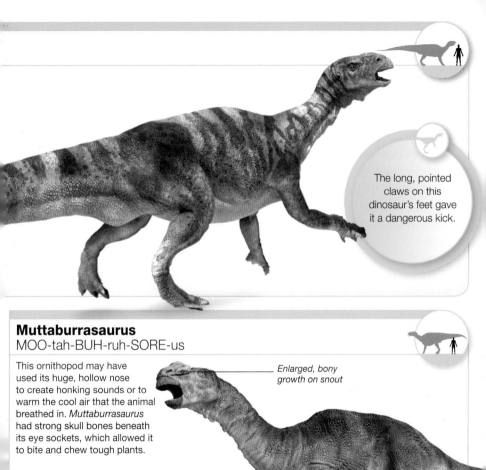

The long, pointed claws on this dinosaur's feet gave it a dangerous kick.

## Muttaburrasaurus
MOO-tah-BUH-ruh-SORE-us

This ornithopod may have used its huge, hollow nose to create honking sounds or to warm the cool air that the animal breathed in. *Muttaburrasaurus* had strong skull bones beneath its eye sockets, which allowed it to bite and chew tough plants.

*Enlarged, bony growth on snout*

**DATE**  100–98 mya (Early Cretaceous)

**SIZE**  26 ft (8 m) long

**FOSSIL LOCATION**  Australia

**HABITAT**  Forests

**DIET**  Plants

***Lesothosaurus*** **was**
# built like a gazelle
**and could easily escape the
bulky predators of the time**

### LESOTHOSAURUS

*Lesothosaurus* lived during the Early Jurassic and was among the earliest ornithopods. It was agile and is seen here evading the crocodilelike predator *Sphenosuchus*. *Lesothosaurus*'s small teeth were shaped like arrowheads, and it probably grazed on low-growing plants.

# Rhabdodon
RAB-doe-don

Although it was discovered in 1869, it is still unclear whether *Rhabdodon* belonged to the hypsilophodont family or the iguanodonts. This broad-bodied ornithopod had stout jaw bones and rounded teeth.

| | |
|---|---|
| **DATE** | 75 mya (Late Cretaceous) |
| **SIZE** | 12 ft (3.7 m) long |
| **FOSSIL LOCATIONS** | Austria, France, Romania, and Spain |
| **HABITAT** | Forests |
| **DIET** | Plants |

# Camptosaurus
CAMP-toe-SORE-us

*Camptosaurus* belonged to the group of ornithopods known as iguanodonts. It was a heavily built animal with a long, horselike face tipped by a beak. Its hands had a thumb spike and the middle fingers supported the weight of the animal's body when on all fours.

| | |
|---|---|
| **DATE** | 155–145 mya (Late Jurassic) |
| **SIZE** | 16½ ft (5 m) long |
| **FOSSIL LOCATION** | United States |
| **HABITAT** | Forests |
| **DIET** | Low-growing herbs and shrubs |

# Iguanodon
ig-GWAH-no-don

*Iguanodon*'s long jaws had leaf-shaped teeth similar to those of a modern-day iguana. It spent most of its time on four legs, feeding on the ground, but could rear up on its hind legs to reach for food on trees. Strong middle toes on its feet supported its weight. In 1825, it became the second prehistoric animal to be identified as a dinosaur, after *Megalosaurus*.

**DATE**  135–125 mya (Early Cretaceous)

**SIZE**  29½–39 ft (9–12 m) long

**FOSSIL LOCATIONS**  Belgium, Germany, France, Spain, and England

**HABITAT**  Forests

**DIET**  Plants

## Maiasaura
MY-a-SORE-a

A fossil site in Montana has remains of numerous bowl-shaped dinosaur nests close to each other. Scientists believe that this was a nesting colony, much like the colonies of modern seabirds, where parents raised their young. They named the nest builders *Maiasaura*, or "good mother lizard."

| | |
|---|---|
| **DATE** | 80–74 mya (Late Cretaceous) |
| **SIZE** | 29½ ft (9 m) long |
| **FOSSIL LOCATION** | United States |
| **HABITAT** | Coastal plains |
| **DIET** | Leaves |

## Hadrosaurus
HAD-roh-SORE-us

This ornithopod used its toothless, beak for tearing twigs and leaves from plants. It had hundreds of blunt teeth at the back of its mouth that ground its food to a pulp.

| | |
|---|---|
| **DATE** | 80–74 mya (Late Cretaceous) |
| **SIZE** | 29½ ft (9 m) long |
| **FOSSIL LOCATION** | North America |
| **HABITAT** | Forests |
| **DIET** | Leaves and twigs |

## Corythosaurus
ko-RITH-oh-SORE-us

The crest of this hadrosaur, or duck-billed dinosaur, looks similar to the helmets worn by the soldiers of Corinth in ancient Greece. This inspired its name. Its crest probably functioned like a trombone, helping it make loud, booming calls to other members of its herd.

| | |
|---|---|
| **DATE** | 76–74 mya (Late Cretaceous) |
| **SIZE** | 29½ ft (9 m) long |
| **FOSSIL LOCATION** | Canada |
| **HABITAT** | Forests and swampy areas |
| **DIET** | Pine needles and seeds |

# Lambeosaurus
LAMB-ee-oh-SORE-us

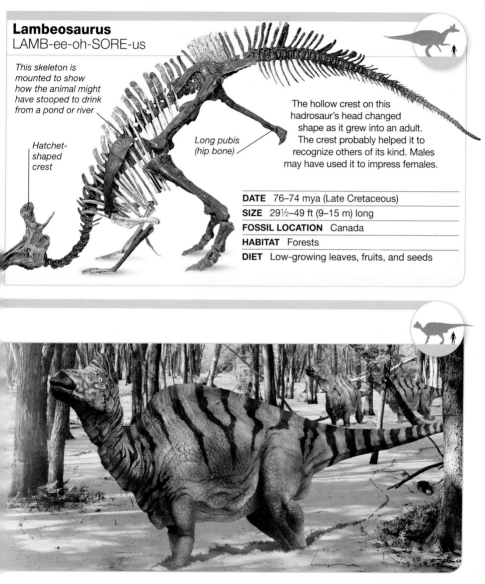

*This skeleton is mounted to show how the animal might have stooped to drink from a pond or river*

*Hatchet-shaped crest*

*Long pubis (hip bone)*

The hollow crest on this hadrosaur's head changed shape as it grew into an adult. The crest probably helped it to recognize others of its kind. Males may have used it to impress females.

| | |
|---|---|
| **DATE** | 76–74 mya (Late Cretaceous) |
| **SIZE** | 29½–49 ft (9–15 m) long |
| **FOSSIL LOCATION** | Canada |
| **HABITAT** | Forests |
| **DIET** | Low-growing leaves, fruits, and seeds |

## Edmontosaurus
ed-MONT-oh-SORE-us

This duck-billed dinosaur had a broad beak, which it used to crop leaves. Then it chewed the food to a pulp with more than 1,000 tiny cheek teeth. Like other hadrosaurs, its hind legs were longer than its forelegs, but it spent most of the time on all fours.

## Brachylophosaurus
BRACK-ee-LOAF-oh-SORE-us

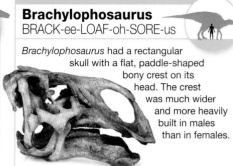

*Brachylophosaurus* had a rectangular skull with a flat, paddle-shaped bony crest on its head. The crest was much wider and more heavily built in males than in females.

| | |
|---|---|
| **DATE** | 76.5 mya (Late Cretaceous) |
| **SIZE** | 29½ ft (9 m) long |
| **FOSSIL LOCATION** | North America |
| **HABITAT** | Forests |
| **DIET** | Ferns, flowering plants, and conifers |

## Parasaurolophus
PA-ra-SORE-oh-LOAF-us

The most striking feature of this dinosaur was the tubelike crest on its head. The cavity within was linked to the animal's nostrils, and *Parasaurolophus* may have used it to make loud, trumpetlike calls to communicate with its herd members.

| | |
|---|---|
| **DATE** | 76–74 mya (Late Cretaceous) |
| **SIZE** | 29½ ft (9 m) long |
| **FOSSIL LOCATION** | North America |
| **HABITAT** | Forests |
| **DIET** | Pine needles and seeds |

| | |
|---|---|
| **DATE** | 75–65 mya (Late Cretaceous) |
| **SIZE** | 43 ft (13 m) long |
| **FOSSIL LOCATIONS** | US and Canada |
| **HABITAT** | Swamps |
| **DIET** | Plants |

Ducklike beak

# Pachycephalosaurs

One of the last groups of dinosaur to evolve was the pachycephalosaurs, or "thick-headed lizards." These dinosaurs get their name from the thick domes on the tops of their skulls. They had many kinds of small, ridged teeth that helped to shred leaves and other vegetation.

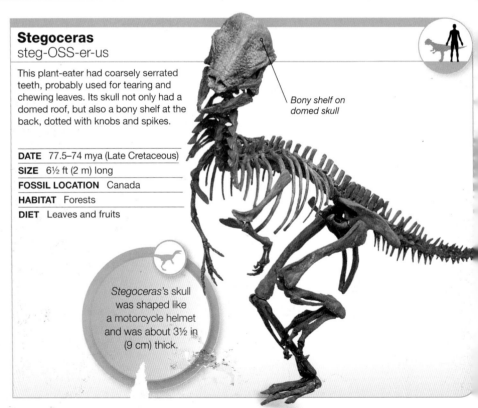

## Stegoceras
steg-OSS-er-us

This plant-eater had coarsely serrated teeth, probably used for tearing and chewing leaves. Its skull not only had a domed roof, but also a bony shelf at the back, dotted with knobs and spikes.

| | |
|---|---|
| **DATE** | 77.5–74 mya (Late Cretaceous) |
| **SIZE** | 6½ ft (2 m) long |
| **FOSSIL LOCATION** | Canada |
| **HABITAT** | Forests |
| **DIET** | Leaves and fruits |

Bony shelf on domed skull

*Stegoceras*'s skull was shaped like a motorcycle helmet and was about 3½ in (9 cm) thick.

# Pachycephalosaurus
PACK-ee-sef-ah-low-SORE-us

The thick skull of this pachycephalosaur was ringed with a crown of bony spikes. The spikes also lined its cheeks and muzzle. The function of this headgear is unknown—rivals may have butted heads or it may have been used to impress mates. *Pachycephalosaurus* had leaflike teeth at the side of its mouth, nipping teeth at front, and conical ones in its lower jaw.

| | |
|---|---|
| **DATE** | 65 mya (Late Cretaceous) |
| **SIZE** | 16½ ft (5 m) long |
| **FOSSIL LOCATION** | North America |
| **HABITAT** | Forests |
| **DIET** | Plants, soft fruits, and seeds |

# Ceratopsians

Although ceratopsians were plant-eaters, their long horns and frills gave them a formidable appearance. Living in herds, they grazed the forests and plains of North America and Asia.

## FOCUS ON... HORNS

Horns evolved from small knobs to formidable weapons.

▲ Early ceratopsians, such as *Psittacosaurus*, had small, bony, hornlike growths on their cheeks.

▲ The main horn of *Centrosaurus* grew over its nose and it used it for defense.

▲ Horns above the eyes not only made *Triceratops* look fierce, but also served as weapons in combat.

## Psittacosaurus
SIT-ack-oh-SORE-us

One of the earliest members of the ceratopsians, *Psittacosaurus* had strong hind legs, which suggest that it could run quickly on only two legs.

**DATE** 120–100 mya (Early Cretaceous)

**SIZE** 6½ ft (2 m) long

**FOSSIL LOCATIONS** China and Mongolia

**HABITAT** Deserts and scrublands

**DIET** Plants

*The dinosaur is asleep in this reconstruction*

# Protoceratops
PRO-toe-SERRA-tops

A small ceratopsian, *Protoceratops* had broad feet and wide, spadelike claws that allowed it to dig burrows for shelter from the desert Sun.

**DATE** 74–65 mya (Late Cretaceous)

**SIZE** 6 ft (1.8 m) long

**FOSSIL LOCATION** Mongolia

**HABITAT** Deserts

**DIET** Desert plants

# Triceratops
try-SERRA-tops

As heavy as a 10-ton truck, this dinosaur was built like a modern rhinoceros. *Tyrannosaurus* bite marks found on *Triceratops* skulls suggest that there were fierce battles between these two species of dinosaur.

**DATE** 70–65 mya (Late Cretaceous)

**SIZE** 29½ ft (9 m) long

**FOSSIL LOCATION** North America

**HABITAT** Forests

**DIET** Forest plants

## Pentaceratops
PEN-ta-SERRA-tops

The most remarkable feature of this dinosaur was its huge head. One fossil skull, built from broken fragments, is more than 10 ft (3 m) long, making it the longest skull of any land animal in history. *Pentaceratops* had five horns on its face, one on the snout, one curved horn on each eyebrow, and a small horn on each cheek.

**DATE**  76–74 mya (Late Cretaceous)

**SIZE**  21½ ft (6.5 m) long

**FOSSIL LOCATION**  United States

**HABITAT**  Forests

**DIET**  Plants

*Eye spots may have enhanced the animal's neck frill display*

## Chasmosaurus
KAZ-mo-SORE-us

An enormous neck frill, which reached over the shoulders, was the most distinctive feature of this dinosaur. Holes present in the frill were covered with brightly colored skin and helped attract mates. *Chasmosaurus* could also tilt its frill upright and startle enemies and predators.

**DATE**  74–65 mya (Late Cretaceous)

**SIZE**  16½ ft (5 m) long

**FOSSIL LOCATION**  North America

**HABITAT**  Forests

**DIET**  Palms and cycads

## Einiosaurus
EYE-nee-oh-SORE-us

The front horn of this dinosaur was very different from that of other ceratopsians. In a young *Einiosaurus,* the horn was straight, but as the animal grew, it gradually curved forward. These dinosaurs lived in herds, moving from place to place to find fresh grazing.

**DATE**  74–65 mya (Late Cretaceous)

**SIZE**  20 ft (6 m) long

**FOSSIL LOCATION**  US

**HABITAT**  Forests

**DIET**  Plants

## Styracosaurus
sty-RACK-oh-SORE-us

Six spikes decorated the frill of this spectacular reptile. The spikes on a male served as a decoration, which attracted females, and the longer the spikes, the more attractive the male looked. The teeth of a *Styracosaurus* grew constantly, replacing worn ones, as the dinosaur munched through the Cretaceous forests.

**DATE**  74–65 mya (Late Cretaceous)

**SIZE**  17 ft (5.2 m) long

**FOSSIL LOCATION**  North America

**HABITAT**  Open woodlands

**DIET**  Ferns and cycads

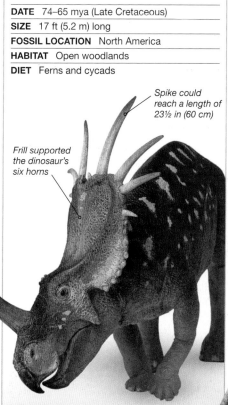

Spike could reach a length of 23½ in (60 cm)

Frill supported the dinosaur's six horns

# Dinosaur neighbors

Dinosaurs were not the only land animals that lived in the Mesozoic Era. They shared the planet with many other creatures. These included other archosaurs, and the rhynchosaurs, cynodonts, and early mammals. These dinosaur neighbors ranged in size from the small, shrewlike mammal *Eomaia* to the dinosaur-sized, bipedal archosaur *Postosuchus* (left).

**EFFIGIA**
Many archosaurs, such as *Effigia*, were similar to dinosaurs, but are more closely related to modern crocodiles and alligators.

# Rhynchosaurs

These barrel-shaped plant-eaters outnumbered dinosaurs during the Triassic. They had a beak at the front of their mouth and several rows of teeth on the mouth's roof. They used tusks to shear plants and then ground and crushed the plant matter before swallowing it.

## Rhynchosaurus
RIN-cho-SORE-us

This reptile had a typical rhynchosaur beak and a deep, broad lower jaw. The skeletons found show that it was well-adapted for fast movement across the ground and had semierect hind limbs. *Rhynchosaurus* used its hind feet to dig out roots and tubers from the soil.

**DATE**   245–240 mya (Middle Triassic)

**SIZE**   1½–3¼ ft (0.5–1 m) long

**FOSSIL LOCATION**   England

**HABITAT**   Semiarid plains

**DIET**   Ferns and tubers

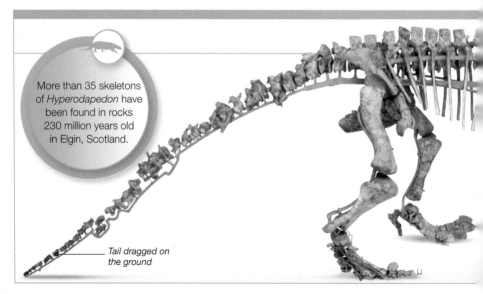

More than 35 skeletons of *Hyperodapedon* have been found in rocks 230 million years old in Elgin, Scotland.

Tail dragged on the ground

## Hyperodapedon
HIGH-per-oh-DAP-eh-don

Like other members of its
group, *Hyperodapedon* was a
heavy-bodied, four-legged plant-eater.
It had a pig-shaped body and a
relatively long tail and its head
was large and deep. Its beak was
curved and it had two short tusks.

*Razor-sharp beak*

| | |
|---|---|
| **DATE** | 231–216 mya (Late Triassic) |
| **SIZE** | 4–5 ft (1.2–1.5 m) long |
| **FOSSIL LOCATIONS** | Scotland, Argentina, Brazil, and India |
| **HABITAT** | Forests |
| **DIET** | Seed ferns and other plants |

# Archosaurs

The first archosaurs evolved around 255 million years ago. From these, an assortment of different animals evolved, including crocodilians, pterosaurs, and dinosaurs.

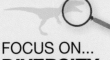
## Stagonolepis
stag-o-NO-lep-iss

*Shovel-like snout*

*Stagonolepis* was one of a group of heavily armored archosaurs called the aetosaurs. Bony armor plates ran the length of its body. It had a short, deep skull that ended in a shovel-like snout, which probably helped it to dig out juicy roots like a pig does today.

| | |
|---|---|
| **DATE** | 235–223 mya (Late Triassic) |
| **SIZE** | 10 ft (3 m) long |
| **FOSSIL LOCATIONS** | Scotland, Poland, and South America |
| **HABITAT** | Forests |
| **DIET** | Horsetails, ferns, and cycads |

▲ Many crurotarsans, such as the crocodilelike *Deinosuchus*, had sprawling limbs.

▲ Others, such as the dinosaur-like *Postosuchus*, could walk on their upright hind limbs.

▲ *Effigia* was even more dinosaurlike, closely resembling the ostrichlike theropods.

# Desmatosuchus
des-MAT-o-SOOK-us

*Desmatosuchus* was an aetosaur that resembled a short-snouted crocodile. It had rows of rectangular bony plates along its back and tail. The underside of part of its belly was also covered with these plates. The spikes on its shoulders could reach a length of 18 in (45 cm).

**DATE** 230 mya (Late Triassic)

**SIZE** 16½ ft (5 m) long

**FOSSIL LOCATION** United States

**HABITAT** Forests

**DIET** Plants

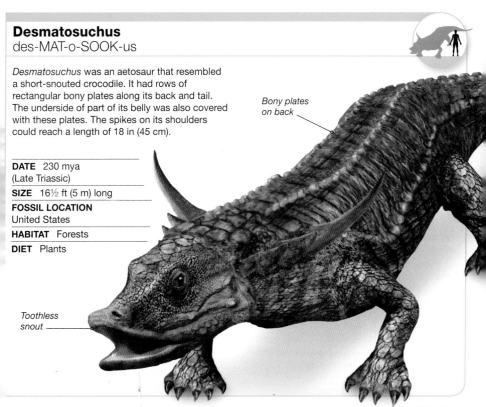

Bony plates on back

Toothless snout

## Lagosuchus
LAG-o-SOOK-us

*Lagosuchus* was an agile archosaur with long, thin hind legs and long feet. These enabled it to chase its prey at great speeds or escape predators quickly.

| | |
|---|---|
| **DATE** | 230 mya (Late Triassic) |
| **SIZE** | 12 in (30 cm) |
| **FOSSIL LOCATION** | Argentina |
| **HABITAT** | Forests |
| **DIET** | Small animals |

## Effigia
eff-IDGE-ee-ah

*Effigia* was a rauisuchian—a type of archosaur with upright legs. Rauisuchians evolved in the Triassic Period. *Effigia* was an omnivore and had a toothless beak like many dinosaurs. It may have used it to crack open seeds and eggs, shear vegetation, or feed on small animals. *Effigia* means "ghost" in Greek—the creature was named after the Ghost Ranch Quarry in New Mexico, where its fossils were found in 1947.

| | |
|---|---|
| **DATE** | 210 mya (Late Triassic) |
| **SIZE** | 6½–10 ft (2–3 m) long |
| **FOSSIL LOCATION** | United States |
| **HABITAT** | Forests |
| **DIET** | Plants, seeds, and animals |

## Parasuchus
para-SOOK-us

*Parasuchus* was a phytosaur—a type of long-snouted archosaur that spent a lot of time in water and resembled today's crocodiles. It hunted for prey near the water's edge. Its eyes faced sideways.

| | |
|---|---|
| **DATE** | 225 mya (Late Triassic) |
| **SIZE** | 6½ ft (2 m) long |
| **FOSSIL LOCATION** | India |
| **HABITAT** | Rivers and swamps |
| **DIET** | Fish and small reptiles |

## Postosuchus
POST-oh-SOOK-us

*Postosuchus* was a large rauisuchian and one of the largest predators of its time. Its large skull had curved, daggerlike teeth that looked like those of the large theropods. It lived alongside the first dinosaurs and probably preyed on them.

**DATE** 230–200 mya (Late Triassic to Early Jurassic)

**SIZE** 14¾ ft (4.5 m) long

**FOSSIL LOCATION** United States

**HABITAT** Forests

**DIET** Small reptiles

# Ornithosuchus
or-nith-oh-SOOK-us

Although it mostly moved around on four limbs, this early archosaur could probably also walk and run on two legs. It used its sharp teeth to slice through the flesh of prey.

**DATE** 230 mya (Late Triassic)

**SIZE** 13 ft (4 m) long

**FOSSIL LOCATION** Scotland

**HABITAT** Swamps of western Europe

**DIET** Small animals

## Dakosaurus
DACK-oh-SORE-us

This distant relative of crocodiles was part of a group of fierce marine predators called the metriorhynchids. Its deep skull resembled that of *Tyrannosaurus*. The skull was lined with sharp teeth that helped *Dakosaurus* to slice through the flesh of other reptiles and crunch the shells of ammonites.

| | |
|---|---|
| **DATE** | 165–140 mya (Late Jurassic) |
| **SIZE** | 13–16½ ft (4–5 m) long |
| **FOSSIL LOCATIONS** | Western Europe, Mexico, and Argentina |
| **HABITAT** | Shallow seas |
| **DIET** | Fish, ammonites, and marine reptiles |

## Terrestrisuchus
teh-REST-rih-SOO-kuss

This tiny carnivore had pencil-thin limb bones and a lightweight skull. It walked with its body raised off the ground. Like modern crocodiles, it had bony plates on its skin.

| | |
|---|---|
| **DATE** | 215–200 mya (Late Triassic) |
| **SIZE** | 2½–3¼ ft (0.75–1 m) long |
| **FOSSIL LOCATIONS** | British Isles, W. Europe |
| **HABITAT** | Dry uplands and forests |
| **DIET** | Insects and small animals |

## Sphenosuchus
SFEN-oh-SOO-kuss

This slender-legged creature could probably run fast when fleeing predators or chasing prey. Parts of its skull had air-filled spaces.

| | |
|---|---|
| **DATE** | 200 mya (Early Jurassic) |
| **SIZE** | 3¼–5 ft (1–1.5 m) long |
| **FOSSIL LOCATION** | South Africa |
| **HABITAT** | Banks of rivers and lakes in humid lowlands |
| **DIET** | Small land animals |

## Deinosuchus
DYE-no-SOO-kuss

*Platelike scales made of bone*

*Deinosuchus* was nearly five times bigger than any alligator found today. It may have lurked patiently at the water's edge, waiting to pounce on passing fish, marine reptiles, or even dinosaurs as large as itself. Much like modern alligators do, it dragged its victims under water and drowned them.

| | |
|---|---|
| **DATE** | 70–65 mya (Late Cretaceous) |
| **SIZE** | 33 ft (10 m) long |
| **FOSSIL LOCATIONS** | United States and Mexico |
| **HABITAT** | Swamps |
| **DIET** | Fish and medium to large dinosaurs |

## Simosuchus
SIGH-moe-SOO-kuss

The name of this creature means "pug-nosed crocodile." Its short skull and blunt face were unusual for a crocodylian. Its teeth suggest that it may have fed mainly on plants. Its hind limbs were semierect and it probably did not run.

| | |
|---|---|
| **DATE** | 70 mya (Late Cretaceous) |
| **SIZE** | 4 ft (1.2 m) long |
| **FOSSIL LOCATION** | Madagascar |
| **HABITAT** | Forests |
| **DIET** | Plants and maybe some insects |

These animals looked like dinosaurs and moved like dinosaurs, but they are **imposters**— members of an earlier group of reptiles called rauisuchians

# Cynodonts and dicynodonts

The cynodonts formed a group of mammal-like reptiles that included the ancestors of modern mammals. Their bodies may have been covered in hair and they walked on upright legs. The cynodonts lived alongside the dicynodonts, which formed another group of mammal-like reptiles with two tusks and a blunt beak.

## FOCUS ON...
## TEETH

Both cynodonts and dicynodonts had distinctive teeth.

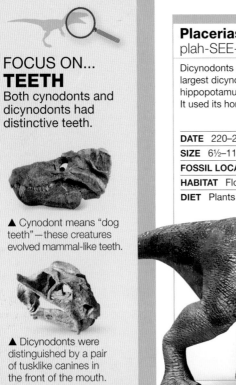

▲ Cynodont means "dog teeth"—these creatures evolved mammal-like teeth.

▲ Dicynodonts were distinguished by a pair of tusklike canines in the front of the mouth.

### Placerias
plah-SEE-ree-ass

Dicynodonts were plant-eaters. *Placerias* was the largest dicynodont in its environment. It looked like a hippopotamus and weighed about 1,300 lb (600 kg). It used its horny beak to shear plants.

**DATE**  220–215 mya (Late Triassic)

**SIZE**  6½–11½ ft (2–3.5 m) long

**FOSSIL LOCATION**  United States

**HABITAT**  Flood plains

**DIET**  Plants

## Lystrosaurus
Lis-trow-SORE-us

Many species of land-living animals died out at the end of the Permian Period. This dicynodont was one of the few animals to survive. *Lystrosaurus* had a piglike, barrel-chested body. Like all dicynodonts, it probably used its canines for display or in defense.

**DATE**  255–230 mya
(Late Permian–Late Triassic)

**SIZE**  3¼ ft (1 m) long

**FOSSIL LOCATIONS**  Africa, Russia, India, China, Mongolia, and Antarctica

**HABITAT**  Dry flood plains

**DIET**  Plants

## Cynognathus
SIGH-nog-NA-thus

The name of this wolf-sized cynodont means "dog-jaw," and it had a large doglike canine on each side of its jaw. It also had bladelike incisors that helped slice flesh. Cynodonts used molar teeth for chewing food, much like their mammal descendants.

**DATE**  247–237 mya (Early–Middle Triassic)

**SIZE**  3¼ ft (1 m) long

**FOSSIL LOCATIONS**  South Africa, Antarctica, and Argentina

**HABITAT**  Forests

**DIET**  Meat

## Thrinaxodon
thrin-AX-oh-don

This catlike predator was the most common cynodont in the early Triassic. It held its limbs almost under its body, like modern mammals do, and it may have had a fur covering.

**DATE**  248–245 mya (Early Triassic)

**SIZE**  12 in (30 cm) long

**FOSSIL LOCATIONS**
South Africa and Antarctica

**HABITAT**
Burrows in forests and riverbanks

**DIET**  Insects and reptiles

# Early mammals

The first mammals evolved in the Triassic Period from cynodont ancestors. These shrewlike early mammals were probably furry and warm-blooded like today's mammals, and many of them may have had a good sense of smell. The early mammals lived alongside the dinosaurs, and the largest of them fed on baby dinosaurs.

## Morganucodon
MORE-gan-YOU-koh-don

This tiny, shrewlike animal was one of the first true mammals. *Morganucodon* had several features typical of its reptilian ancestors, including a double jaw joint. It probably laid eggs as reptiles do and actively hunted at night. It was discovered in 1949 in Wales.

| | |
|---|---|
| **DATE** | 210–180 mya (Late Triassic–Early Jurassic) |
| **SIZE** | 3½ in (9 cm) long |
| **FOSSIL LOCATIONS** | Wales, China, and US |
| **HABITAT** | Forests |
| **DIET** | Insects |

Sharp teeth

## Nemegtbaatar
nem-EGT-bat-or

Wide snout

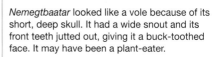

*Nemegtbaatar* looked like a vole because of its short, deep skull. It had a wide snout and its front teeth jutted out, giving it a buck-toothed face. It may have been a plant-eater.

| | |
|---|---|
| **DATE** | 65 mya (Late Cretaceous) |
| **SIZE** | 4 in (10 cm) long |
| **FOSSIL LOCATION** | Mongolia |
| **HABITAT** | Forests |
| **DIET** | Possibly plants |

## Megazostrodon
MEG-ah-ZO-stroh-don

This animal had a slender body, with a long snout and tail. It probably burrowed and ran like today's rats and shrews. Each of its cheek teeth had short, triangular points, possibly used for cutting up insects.

**DATE**  190 mya (Early Jurassic)

**SIZE**  4 in (10 cm) long

**FOSSIL LOCATION**  South Africa

**HABITAT**  Forests

**DIET**  Insects

## Eomaia
EE-oh-MY-ah

Rat-sized *Eomaia*'s name stands for "dawn mother." It was one of the first placental mammals, the large group of modern mammals with a placenta—a structure inside the mother's body that nourishes the developing young.

**DATE**  125 mya (Early Cretaceous)

**SIZE**  8 in (20 cm) long

**FOSSIL LOCATION**  China

**HABITAT**  Forests

**DIET**  Insects and other small animals

## Sinoconodon
SIGH-no-CON-oh-don

*Sinoconodon* was the size of a squirrel. It had a strong jaw joint and chin and may have had a powerful bite. Its ear bones were like those of a mammal, but its teeth were replaced throughout life, as in a reptile.

**DATE**  200 mya (Early Jurassic)

**SIZE**  12 in (30 cm) long

**FOSSIL LOCATION**  China

**HABITAT**  Forests

**DIET**  Omnivorous

# Sea reptiles

While dinosaurs were the dominant life forms on land, the oceans were ruled by gigantic predatory reptiles, which included the plesiosaurs, nothosaurs, and mosasaurs (left). These reptiles used their flipper-shaped limbs to surge rapidly through the ocean, often chasing prey. Many of them had pointed teeth that held on to slippery fish.

**TURTLES**
Aside from monstrous predators, other marine reptiles included the placodonts and turtles, like *Protostega*, which developed thick defensive plates on its back.

# Placodonts and turtles

During the Middle Triassic Period, shallow coastal seas covering Europe teemed with predatory reptiles called placodonts. They had a large, barrel-chested body, webbed limbs that worked as paddles, and a long, deep tail. The earliest turtles also lived around the same time. They had a short skull, a tiny tail, and a protective shell.

## Placodus
plak-OH-dus

This reptile was an expert swimmer, despite its bulky body. Unusually for a reptile, it had protruding front teeth that probably speared fish. Peglike teeth on the roof of its mouth would have crushed the hard shells of mollusks.

| | |
|---|---|
| **DATE** | 245–235 mya (Middle Triassic) |
| **SIZE** | 6½–10 ft (2–3 m) long |
| **FOSSIL LOCATION** | Germany |
| **HABITAT** | Shallow seas near reefs |
| **DIET** | Mussels, fish, and other invertebrates |

## Kayentachelys
ka-YEN-ta-KEE-lis

*Kayentachelys* was among the first turtles to evolve the fully formed, boxlike protective shell seen in modern species. It had a sharp beak like its modern relatives and like most of today's turtles, it could pull in its head and limbs to hide within the protective shell, if needed.

| | |
|---|---|
| **DATE** | 196–183 mya (Early Jurassic) |
| **SIZE** | 23½ in (60 cm) long |
| **FOSSIL LOCATION** | United States |
| **HABITAT** | Near streams in arid regions |
| **DIET** | Plants and animals |

# Odontochelys
oh-DON-toh-KEE-lis

*Odontochelys* is the most ancient and primitive turtle discovered so far.

*Odontochelys* differed from modern turtles in two major ways. Today's turtles have a toothless beak, while this ancestral creature had jaws lined with teeth. This inspired its name, which means "toothed turtle." It also had a shell that covered only its belly, unlike those of modern turtles, which protect both the belly and the back.

| | |
|---|---|
| **DATE** | 220 mya (Late Triassic) |
| **SIZE** | 16 in (40 cm) long |
| **FOSSIL LOCATION** | China |
| **HABITAT** | Shallow coastal seas |
| **DIET** | Fish, ammonites, and plants |

# Nothosaurs

The nothosaurs patrolled the shallow coastal seas of the Triassic at about the same time as the first dinosaurs appeared on land. These fish-hunters had four legs with webbed feet and probably bred on beaches and coastal rocks, much like seals do today.

## Pachypleurosaurus
PACK-ee-ploo-roe-SORE-us

*Pachypleurosaurus* was a small animal with a snakelike, streamlined body and a long tail. It swam like an otter—by moving its body in a wavelike pattern—and steered with the help of paddlelike hind limbs.

| | |
|---|---|
| **DATE** | 225 mya (Late Triassic) |
| **SIZE** | 12–16 in (30–40 cm) long |
| **FOSSIL LOCATIONS** | Italy and Switzerland |
| **HABITAT** | Shallow oceans |
| **DIET** | Small fish |

## Lariosaurus
LA-ree-oh-SORE-us

A small nothosaur, *Lariosaurus* lived mainly in water, but often came out onto land. Unlike most reptiles, this nothosaur probably gave birth to live young.

| | |
|---|---|
| **DATE** | 234–227 mya (Late Triassic) |
| **SIZE** | 20–28 in (50–70 cm) long |
| **FOSSIL LOCATION** | Italy |
| **HABITAT** | Shallow oceans |
| **DIET** | Small fish and shrimp |

# Nothosaurus
NO-tho-SORE-us

Like other nothosaurs, *Nothosaurus* probably swam by waving its long body and tail to move through water. Its long, pointed teeth were good at gripping slippery prey. Much like crocodiles, it could throw its head to one side to seize passing fish.

**DATE** 240–210 mya (Middle–Late Triassic)

**SIZE** 4–13 ft (1.2–4 m) long

**FOSSIL LOCATIONS** Europe, Africa, Russia, and China

**HABITAT** Shallow oceans

**DIET** Fish and shrimp

# Ichthyosaurs

The oceans of the Mesozoic Era were home to many predatory reptiles, including this group of dolphinlike beasts. Streamlined hunters, the ichthyosaurs swam using their sharklike fins and tails and fed on squid, ammonites, fish, and marine reptiles. They had large eyes and gave birth to young in water.

### Shonisaurus
SHON-ee-SORE-us

*Shonisaurus* had a long, toothless snout. When catching prey, strong muscles in the mouth pulled its tongue back rapidly, helping to suck in its victims. It was the largest marine reptile ever to live on the Earth.

| | |
|---|---|
| **DATE** | 225–208 mya (Late Triassic) |
| **SIZE** | Up to 69 ft (21 m) long |
| **FOSSIL LOCATION** | North America |
| **HABITAT** | Open oceans |
| **DIET** | Fish and squid |

# Ichthyosaurus
ICK-thee-oh-SORE-us

A small predator, *Ichthyosaurus* could catch fast-moving, slippery prey—its snout was long and armed with banks of sharp, needlelike teeth. Like all ichthyosaurs, it hunted mainly using eyesight. Its large eyes were protected by bony shields.

| | |
|---|---|
| **DATE** | 190 mya (Early Jurassic) |
| **SIZE** | 6½ ft (2 m) long |
| **FOSSIL LOCATIONS** | British Isles, Belgium, and Germany |
| **HABITAT** | Open oceans |
| **DIET** | Fish and squid |

## Mixosaurus
MIX-oh-SORE-us

*Mixosaurus* was an early ichthyosaur and like others of its kind, it swam by beating its tail from side to side, probably using bursts of speed to chase after or surge through shoals of fish.

| | |
|---|---|
| **DATE** | 230 mya (Late Triassic) |
| **SIZE** | Up to 3¼ ft (1 m) long |
| **FOSSIL LOCATIONS** | North America, Europe, Asia |
| **HABITAT** | Open oceans |
| **DIET** | Fish |

## Temnodontosaurus
tem-NOH-don-toh-SORE-us

This large ichthyosaur could dive to great depths in the seas when hunting for prey. Its eyes had a diameter of 8 in (20 cm), making them larger than those of most other vertebrates.

| | |
|---|---|
| **DATE** | 198–185 mya (Early Jurassic) |
| **SIZE** | 39 ft (12 m) long |
| **FOSSIL LOCATIONS** | England and Germany |
| **HABITAT** | Shallow seas |
| **DIET** | Fish and squid |

# Plesiosaurs

Fully adapted to an aquatic life, these gigantic carnivorous reptiles dominated the oceans in the Jurassic and Cretaceous periods, swimming in the water with four long flippers. Many of them had long, snakelike necks and small heads.

## Cryptoclidus
KRIP-toe-KLIDE-us

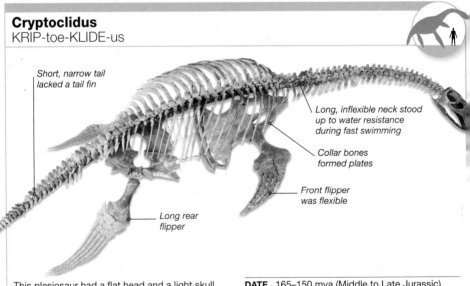

Short, narrow tail lacked a tail fin

Long, inflexible neck stood up to water resistance during fast swimming

Collar bones formed plates

Front flipper was flexible

Long rear flipper

This plesiosaur had a flat head and a light skull. It had hundreds of teeth, which interlocked with each other and trapped fish and other small marine animals. Like other plesiosaurs, it probably "flew" through water, moving its flippers like wings. Some scientists think that it may have come ashore to lay eggs.

| | |
|---|---|
| **DATE** | 165–150 mya (Middle to Late Jurassic) |
| **SIZE** | 26 ft (8 m) long |
| **FOSSIL LOCATIONS** | England, France, Russia, and South America |
| **HABITAT** | Shallow oceans |
| **DIET** | Fish and squid |

# Elasmosaurus
el-LAZZ-moe-SORE-us

A fish-eater, *Elasmosaurus* probably swam over the seabed, reaching down to grab prey. Its neck was supported by 72 vertebrae (spine bones)—more than that in any other animal that has ever lived.

**DATE** 99–65 mya (Late Cretaceous)

**SIZE** 46 ft (14 m) long

**FOSSIL LOCATION** United States

**HABITAT** Open oceans

**DIET** Fish, squid, and ammonites

# Plesiosaurus
PLEE-see-oh-SORE-us

*Plesiosaurus* had a wide, turtlelike body. It may have hunted by swimming among shoals of fish, swinging its long neck from side to side to catch prey. It had wide, U-shaped jaws and sharp, conical teeth that gripped prey.

**DATE** 200 mya (Early Jurassic)

**SIZE** 10–16½ ft (3–5 m) long

**FOSSIL LOCATIONS** British Isles and Germany

**HABITAT** Open oceans

**DIET** Fish and ammonites

Ribs in the middle of the trunk

# Pliosaurs

Plesiosaurs with short necks and large heads, the pliosaurs were some of the most formidable predators ever to swim in the Earth's oceans. With muscular necks, huge jaws, and crocodilelike teeth, these sea monsters attacked and ate any creature they swam into. Their main foes were gigantic sharks and others of their own kind.

## Liopleurodon
LIE-oh-PLOOR-oh-don

Liopleurodon's jaws were very powerful and it may have had a stronger bite than *Tyrannosaurus*. Scientists think that this creature had a keen sense of smell that enabled it to hunt in deep waters where prey was difficult to spot. Its long, paddlelike flippers suggest that it swam at high speeds in short spurts.

| | |
|---|---|
| **DATE** | 165–150 mya (Middle to Late Jurassic) |
| **SIZE** | 16½–23 ft (5–7 m) long |
| **FOSSIL LOCATIONS** | British Isles, Germany, France, and Russia |
| **HABITAT** | Open oceans |
| **DIET** | Large squid and ichthyosaurs |

# Rhomaleosaurus
ROME-alley-oh-SORE-us

This pliosaur had a good sense of smell and could pick up the scent of prey from far away. It also had sharp eyesight, allowing it to hunt at close range. Once it had seized prey, it probably twisted around in the water to rip its victim apart, much like crocodiles do.

**DATE** 200–195 mya (Early Jurassic)

**SIZE** 16½–23 ft (5–7 m) long

**FOSSIL LOCATIONS** England and Germany

**HABITAT** Coastal waters

**DIET** Fish, squid, and ocean reptiles

# Kronosaurus
crow-no-SORE-us

Like a modern crocodile, *Kronosaurus* could open its jaws wide to seize prey. The head of this monstrous predator was about 10 ft (3 m) long and larger than a man. Its skull was nearly twice the size of a *Tyrannosaurus* skull.

**DATE** 65 mya (Late Cretaceous)

**SIZE** 33 ft (10 m) long

**FOSSIL LOCATIONS** Australia and Colombia

**HABITAT** Open oceans

**DIET** Marine reptiles, fish, and ammonites

*Rhomaleosaurus*
rushed in to
# cripple
# its prey
**with a series of massive
bites, rather like a
great white shark**

### RHOMALEOSAURUS

*Rhomaelosaurus* was a pliosaur that preyed on fish, ichthyosaurs, and smaller plesiosaurs. Like all plesiosaurs, it could smell prey from far away by channeling water to sense organs above the roof of its mouth. These detected scents, then the water drained out through its nostrils.

# Mosasaurs

Colossal lizards called mosasaurs were major predators in Late Cretaceous seas. They evolved from small land-dwelling lizards that took to the water. Fully adapted to marine life, they had paddlelike limbs and swam like crocodiles.

## Mosasaurus
MOZE-ah-SORE-us

This crocodilelike hunter swam by moving its long body in slow waves and probably hunted slow-moving prey in the surface waters of the oceans. It could even overpower plesiosaurs.

| | |
|---|---|
| **DATE** | 70–65 mya (Late Cretaceous) |
| **SIZE** | 49–57¾ ft (15–17.6 m) long |
| **FOSSIL LOCATIONS** | US, Belgium, Japan, Netherlands, New Zealand, Morocco, and Turkey |
| **HABITAT** | Shallow coastal oceans |
| **DIET** | Fish, squid, plesiosaurs, and shellfish |

# Plioplatecarpus
PLEE-o-PLAH-teh-CAR-pus

This midsized predator preferred warm and shallow oceans. The shape of its teeth and skull suggests that it probably hunted small prey. Its long skull was equipped with thick, conical teeth. It had larger eyes than other mosasaurs.

| | |
|---|---|
| **DATE** | 83.5 mya (Late Cretaceous) |
| **SIZE** | 16½–20 ft (5–6 m) long |
| **FOSSIL LOCATIONS** | Europe, Canada, and United States |
| **HABITAT** | Shallow oceans |
| **DIET** | Fish |

# Flying reptiles

The Mesozoic Era saw the evolution and extinction of some extraordinary flying reptiles. These were the pterosaurs, which first took to the skies in the Triassic and by the end of the Cretaceous had reached colossal proportions. Pterosaurs included the agile *Pterodactylus*, which snatched fish out of the oceans as well as the gigantic *Quetzalcoatlus* (left), which stalked through Cretaceous forests, preying on dinosaurs.

**PTERODACTYLUS**
A Jurassic pterosaur, *Pterodactylus* lived near coasts, hunting during the day and sleeping at night.

# Pterosaurs

The reptiles that took to the air in the Triassic were a type of archosaur called pterosaurs and some were the largest creatures ever to fly. They had batlike wings made of skin and their bodies were covered in fur.

FOCUS ON...
## TAILS
The aerodynamics of pterosaurs improved during their evolution.

### Rhamphorhynchus
ram-foe-RINK-us

This pterosaur had a long, bony tail. The tail had a diamond-shaped flap of skin at the end that may have worked like a rudder, helping this reptile steer.

| | |
|---|---|
| **DATE** | 150 mya (Late Jurassic) |
| **SIZE** | 1–6 ft (0.3–1.8 m) wingspan |
| **FOSSIL LOCATIONS** | Europe and Africa |
| **HABITAT** | Coasts and riverbanks |
| **DIET** | Fish |

▲ Typical Triassic pterosaurs, such as *Eudimorphodon*, had long tails and short legs and wings. They belonged to a group called the rhamphorhynchoids.

▲ A new group called the pterodactyloids evolved in the Jurassic. Their shorter tails and longer wings made them more agile in the air.

## Dimorphodon
die-MORE-foe-don

This creature's huge head was almost one-third of its body length. Unusually for a pterosaur, it had two types of teeth. Longer teeth in the front helped snap up prey, while the ones at the back were used to grind food.

| | |
|---|---|
| **DATE** | 200–180 mya (Early Jurassic) |
| **SIZE** | 4¾ ft (1.45 m) wingspan |
| **FOSSIL LOCATION** | British Isles |
| **HABITAT** | Coastal forests |
| **DIET** | Fish and small, lizardlike reptiles |

## Peteinosaurus
pet-INE-oh-SORE-us

This reptile's name means "winged lizard." The wings of this early pterosaur were far smaller than those of the Cretaceous pterosaurs, such as *Pteranodon*.

| | |
|---|---|
| **DATE** | 228–215 mya (Late Triassic) |
| **SIZE** | 23½ in (60 cm) wingspan |
| **FOSSIL LOCATION** | Italy |
| **HABITAT** | Swamps and river valleys |
| **DIET** | Flying insects |

## Anurognathus
an-YOOR-og-NATH-us

This tiny pterosaur may have fed on damselflies and lacewings. It probably landed on the backs of the sauropods before attacking the insects flying near them.

| | |
|---|---|
| **DATE** | 150–145 mya (Late Jurassic) |
| **SIZE** | 20 in (50.8 cm) wingspan |
| **FOSSIL LOCATION** | Germany |
| **HABITAT** | Forests |
| **DIET** | Flying insects |

The small crest on *Pterodactylus*'s head was made from bone and thick skin and was probably used for display.

# Pterodactylus
TEH-roe-DACK-till-us

Many complete fossils of *Pterodactylus* have been found, making it the best-known of all pterosaurs. It had a much smaller tail and longer wing bones than earlier pterosaurs, making it far more agile in flight.

| | |
|---|---|
| **DATE** | 150–144 mya (Late Jurassic) |
| **SIZE** | 3¼ ft (1 m) wingspan |
| **FOSSIL LOCATION** | Germany |
| **HABITAT** | Coastal areas |
| **DIET** | Fish, insects, and perhaps carrion |

# Quetzalcoatlus
KWETS-ul-coe-AT-luss

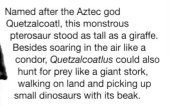

Named after the Aztec god Quetzalcoatl, this monstrous pterosaur stood as tall as a giraffe. Besides soaring in the air like a condor, *Quetzalcoatlus* could also hunt for prey like a giant stork, walking on land and picking up small dinosaurs with its beak.

**DATE** 70–65 mya (Late Cretaceous)

**SIZE** 33–36 ft (10–11 m) wingspan

**FOSSIL LOCATION** United States

**HABITAT** Open plains and forests

**DIET** Mammals, lizards, and dinosaurs

*Quetzalcoatlus* weighed about 20 times as much as today's heaviest flying birds—an amazing 530 lb (240 kg).

## Tupandactylus
TU-PAN-dac-TI-luss

The large
fanlike crest
of this animal
was the largest of
all known pterosaur
crests, relative to the
creature's head size.
The crest was held
aloft by thin bony rods.

**DATE** 112 mya (Early Cretaceous)

**SIZE** 8¼ ft (2.5 m) wingspan

**FOSSIL LOCATION** Brazil

**HABITAT** Coasts

**DIET** Possibly fish

## Ornithocheirus
Or-NITH-oh-KEE-rus

Scientists do not know much about this creature
because very few fossils have been found. After
studying the fossil fragments, scientists estimate
that *Ornithocheirus* had a wingspan of 33 ft
(10 m) and there was a bony bump at the end
of its snout, which it probably used for display.

**DATE** 110 mya (Early Cretaceous)

**SIZE** 26–33 ft (8–10 m) wingspan

**FOSSIL LOCATIONS** Europe and South America

**HABITAT** Coasts

**DIET** Fish

# Prehistoric records

## DINOSAUR RECORDS

▶ **Longest neck relative to body size**
In 2002, researchers working in Mongolia dug up six vertebrae, along with part of a breastbone and several leg bones of a previously unknown sauropod, which was called *Erketu ellisoni*. Based on its vertebrae, scientists estimated that its neck was 26 ft (8 m) long, making it the longest neck, relative to body size, of any known land animal.

▶ **Tallest dinosaur** The tallest of all dinosaurs was the sauropod *Sauroposeidon*. Although it was shorter in length than other sauropods, its neck allowed it to reach heights of up to 59 ft (18 m)—higher than any other sauropod.

▶ **Longest bone** The longest bone of any dinosaur belongs to a sauropod called *Ultrasaurus*. The bone was its shoulder blade and measured 8¼ ft (2.4 m) in length.

▶ **Brainiest dinosaur** The brainiest of all dinosaurs was *Troodon*. Relative to its body size, this theropod had the largest brain.

▶ **Largest skull** The ceratopsian *Pentaceratops* holds the distinction of having the largest skull of any land animal—it measured 10 ft (3 m) long.

▶ **Thickest skull** *Pachycephalosaurus*, an ornithischian, had the thickest skull of all dinosaurs. A bony dome on top of the skull was 8 in (20 cm) thick.

▶ **Longest claws** The theropod *Deinocheirus* had the longest claws of any dinosaur. Each claw measured up to 7¾ in (19.6 cm) long.

▶ **Most Teeth** Of all the dinosaurs, the hadrosaur *Shantungosaurus* had the greatest number of teeth. It had more than 1,500 chewing teeth at the back of its mouth—these helped it to chew its plant food to a pulp.

## PTEROSAUR RECORDS

★ **Largest pterosaur** With a wingspan of more than 36 ft (11 m), *Quetzalcoatlus* was the largest flying reptile of all time.

★ **Smallest pterosaur** *Nemicolopterus* had a wingspan of only 10 in (25 cm), making it the smallest pterosaur.

★ **Largest head crest** Relative to its body size, *Tupandactylus* had the largest head crest of all pterosaurs.

# MARINE REPTILE RECORDS

★ **Largest ichthyosaur** *Shonisaurus* was the largest ichthyosaur. It lived in the Triassic Period and could reach lengths of up to 69 ft (21 m).

★ **Smallest ichthyosaur** The smallest ichthyosaur was *Chaohusaurus*. It measured only 6 ft (1.8 m) in length—the height of an average man.

★ **Largest plesiosaur** With a body length of more than 66 ft (20 m), *Mauisaurus* was the largest plesiosaur.

★ **Shortest plesiosaur** *Umoonasaurus* grew to a length of 8¼ ft (2.5 m) and was the smallest plesiosaur.

★ **Largest pliosaur** *Kronosaurus* was the largest of all pliosaurs. It measured up to 33 ft (10 m) in length.

★ **Smallest pliosaur** The smallest pliosaur skeleton found so far is that of *Leptocleidus*. This reptile was only 5 ft (1.5 m) in length.

★ **Largest mosasaur** *Mosasaurus* could reach lengths of up to 57¾ ft (17.6 m), making it the largest mosasaur.

★ **Smallest mosasaur** *Carinodens* was the smallest of all mosasaurs, although it was still quite a moster, measuring 11½ ft (3.5 m) long.

# OLDEST CREATURES

• **Oldest reptile** The fossils of *Hylonomus lyelli* are older than that of any other reptile. This creature lived 312 million years ago, in the Carboniferous Period. This ancient reptile was only about 8 in (20 cm) long.

• **Oldest archosaur** *Archosaurus* lived in Russia in the Late Permian Period, around 255 million years ago, and is older than any other archosaur.

• **Oldest dinosaur** In 2011, scientists discovered fossils of *Eodromaeus*. These fossils have been dated to be more than 232 million years old—making this the oldest dinosaur found so far.

• **Oldest bird** Until recently, experts thought of *Archaeopteryx* as the oldest known bird. However, recent research by a team of Chinese scientists may change this fact. A feathered theropod called *Xiaotingia zhengi*, which lived around 155 million years ago, may have been more closely related to birds and could soon be confirmed as the earliest bird.

• **Oldest mammal** *Adelobasileus* lived in North America in the Late Triassic Period, around 220 million years ago. It is the oldest mammal.

# Largest dinosaurs

Among the dinosaurs, there were some that reached gigantic proportions. Scientists are still not sure why this happened, but there are many advantages in being huge. For the largest plant-eating dinosaurs, it meant that even the most ferocious predators may have failed to bring them down. In the sauropods, gigantic digestive systems also helped to extract nutrients efficiently from plant food. Many theropods also grew larger and were able to hunt larger prey. While giant animals may live longer than small ones, they need a great amount of food, and so are vulnerable to sudden changes in climate or food supply.

## LONGEST SAUROPODS

The longest sauropods were also the largest-ever land animals, therefore also the biggest dinosaurs.

❶ *Argentinosaurus* lived in the Cretaceous Period. Scientists have found only fragments of its bones, which include vertebrae, ribs, and a thigh bone. Using these bones, they estimated that this sauropod measured between 108–134 ft (33–41 m) from head to tail.

❷ *Supersaurus* was a Jurassic sauropod and a relative of *Apatosaurus*. Fossil remains suggest that it would have reached lengths of 108–112 ft (33–34 m).

❸ *Sauroposeidon* is probably one of the last of the gigantic sauropods to live in North America. This Cretaceous dinosaur could reach a length of 92–112 ft (28–34 m). This sauropod is known from four neck vertebrae, which suggest that it was similar to *Brachiosaurus*.

❹ *Futalognkosaurus* was discovered in 2000. This Cretaceous sauropod could reach 92–112 ft (28–34 m) in length, the same as *Sauroposeidon*.

❺ *Diplodocus* lived toward the end of the Jurassic Period. It could reach lengths from 98½ ft (30 m) to 110 ft (33.5 m).

❻ *Paralititan* is a little known Cretaceous sauropod. However, by comparing it with its relative *Saltasaurus*, scientists have estimated that it measured up to 105 ft (32 m) in length.

❼ *Turiasaurus* was the largest sauropod in Europe, measuring more than 98½ ft (30 m) in length.

# LONGEST THEROPODS

These dinosaurs were also the world's largest-ever land predators.

❶ **Spinosaurus** was a Cretaceous theropod weighing about 7 tons and measuring 59 ft (18 m) in length.

❷ **Carcharodontosaurus** could weigh as much as 8 tons and reach a total length of more than 46 ft (14 m).

❸ **Giganotosaurus** lived in the late Cretaceous Period. This theropod could grow to a length of 43 ft (13 m).

❹ **Tyrannotitan** could grow up to 40 ft (12.2 m), making it slightly larger than *Tyrannosaurus*.

❺ **Tyrannosaurus** is the best-known of all giant theropods. It could reach 39 ft (12 m) in length and weighed more than 6 tons.

❻ **Zhuchengtyrannus** was a cousin of *Tyrannosaurus* and lived in China during the Cretaceous Period. It could measure up to 36 ft (11 m) in length and weighed more than 6½ tons.

# LONGEST ORNITHOPODS

❶ **Shantungosaurus** lived in the Cretaceous Period. This ornithopod measured more than 52½ ft (16 m) in length.

❷ **Lambeosaurus** is best known for its distinctive hollow crest on top of its head. It could reach a length of 49 ft (15 m).

Although some theropods were the largest predators on land, others, such as *Microraptor gui* were among the smallest of all dinosaurs.

❸ **Edmontosaurus** was a duck-billed ornithopod, measuring up to 43 ft (13 m) long.

❹ **Charonosaurus** was discovered in 2000. Its fossils were found near a riverbank in China. Scientists estimated that this dinosaur could grow to 43 ft (13 m) in length.

❺ **Iguanodon** lived from the Late Jurassic Period to the Early Cretaceous Period. This ornithopod could reach lengths of more than 39 ft (12 m).

❻ **Olorotitan** was found as a complete fossil skeleton in 2003. This dinosaur could grow to up to 39 ft (12 m).

❼ **Saurolophus** had a body length of 39 ft (12 m).

# Dinosaur discoveries

People have been discovering dinosaur bones for centuries. These bones were once thought to be of mythical creatures, and this may have given rise to the legends of dragons and giants told in different parts of the world. From the 1700s, scientists began studying these bones as evidence of animals that lived before the appearance of humans.

## GREAT PALEONTOLOGISTS

Scientists who study dinosaurs and other prehistoric animals are known as paleontologists. Their research and discoveries allow us to understand prehistoric life.

▶ **Othniel C. Marsh (1831–99) and Edward Drinker Cope (1840–97)** were rival paleontologists who discovered many dinosaurs, including *Triceratops* and *Diplodocus*.

▶ **Harry Govier Seeley (1839–1909)** was a British paleontologist who classified dinosaurs into saurischians and ornithischians, based on the arrangements of their hip bones.

▶ **Barnum Brown (1873–1963)** was an American fossil hunter who was the first to discover fossils of *Tyrannosaurus*.

▶ **Elmer S. Riggs (1869–1963)** was an American paleontologist who named and described the sauropod *Brachiosaurus*, two years after its fossils were discovered.

▶ **Ernst Stromer von Reichenbach (1870–1952)** was a German paleontologist who named the 59-ft- (18-m-) long *Spinosaurus*.

▶ **Roy Chapman Andrews (1884–1960)** was an American explorer who led a number of expeditions to the Gobi Desert in Mongolia. His team discovered fossils of *Oviraptor*, *Velociraptor*, and *Proceratops*, as well as dinosaur eggs.

▶ **Alan Charig (1927–97)** was an American paleontologist who figured out how dinosaurs evolved from archosaurs.

▶ **Robert Bakker (b. 1945)** is an American paleontologist who put forward the theories that dinosaurs were warm-blooded animals and gave rise to birds.

▶ **John "Jack" Horner (b. 1946) and Robert Makela (1940–87)** were a team of American paleontologists who excavated dinosaur nests and found evidence that dinosaurs cared for their young.

# GREAT DISCOVERIES

Since the 1600s, paleontologists have found and named more than 600 different dinosaurs. Some of the major milestones in the search for dinosaurs are given below.

**1811** Mary Anning was just 11 years old when she became the first person to find the fossils of an ichthyosaur, in the cliffs of Lyme Regis in England. She was also the first to find a plesiosaur fossil, 12 years later.

**1820** Gideon Mantell began collecting fossils of a dinosaur that he would later name *Iguanodon.* His attempts to study and reconstruct the structure and living habits of this animal spurred the scientific study of dinosaurs.

**1824** *Megalosaurus* became the first dinosaur to be named scientifically.

**1842** Sir Richard Owens coined the term "Dinosauria," which means terrible lizard.

**1856** *Troodon* became the first American dinosaur to be given a scientific name.

**In 1861** German paleontologist Hermann von Meyer published a paper in which he described *Archaeopteryx*, which came to be considered the first bird.

**1877** Huge fossil finds in Colorado began a dinosaur rush, leading to the discovery of *Allosaurus*, *Apatosaurus*, *Diplodocus*, *Triceratops*, and *Stegosaurus.*

**1908–12** German paleontologists Werner Janensch and Edwin Hennig found fossils of *Brachiosaurus* and *Kentrosaurus* in Tanzania, Africa.

**1933–70s** Chinese paleontologist Yang Zhongjian oversaw fossil discoveries in China and named many dinosaurs, including *Lufengosaurus*, *Mamenchisaurus*, *Omeisaurus*, and *Tsintaosaurus*.

More than 486 dinosaurs have been named in the last 20 years.

**1979** American geologist Walter Alvarez and his father Luis Alvarez put forward the theory that the collision of an asteroid or comet with the Earth led to the extinction of the dinosaurs.

**1991** American paleontologist William Hammer discovered *Cryolophosaurus* in the Antarctic, making it the first theropod to be discovered on that continent.

**1998** Chinese paleontologists Chen Pei-ji, Dong Zhi-ming, and Zhen Shou-nan found *Sinosauropteryx*, the first dinosaur known to have a feathered body.

# Glossary

**3-D** Having three dimensions (length, height, and depth), either in the real world, or in the virtual world of computer models or graphics.

**Aetosaurs** A group of plant-eating archosaurs from the Triassic Period. Aetosaurs had armored plates and spines on their backs.

**Ammonites** An extinct group of mollusks related to squid. They had a coiled shell and lived in Mesozoic seas.

**Amphibian** A vertebrate animal such as a frog that usually starts life in water as a tadpole, but turns into an air-breathing adult that lives partly on land.

**Ancestor** An animal or plant species from which a more recent species has evolved.

**Angiosperms** The plant group that contains flowering plants. This group includes broad-leaved trees and grasses.

**Ankylosaurs** A group of four-legged, armored, plant-eating ornithischian dinosaurs with bony plates covering the neck, shoulder, and back, and a bony club at the end of the tail.

**Archosaurs** A group of prehistoric reptiles that include the dinosaurs, pterosaurs, and crocodilians and their relatives. The archosaurs had a distinctive cavity in the skull on each side of the snout between the eye and the nostril. They evolved around 255 million years ago.

**Arid** Describes a dry climate or place.

**Asteroid** A large rocky object that orbits the Sun—bigger than a meteoroid but smaller than a planet.

**Asymmetrical** Having unequal parts.

**Binocular vision** Viewing a scene or object with two eyes. This enables an animal to judge distance to the scene or object.

**Bipedal** Describes animals that walk on two hind limbs.

**Bird** A feathered theropod dinosaur capable of powered flight or an animal descended from such a flying ancestor.

**Brackish** Water that is saltier than fresh water, but less salty than ocean water.

**Cambrian** The first period of the Paleozoic Era, lasting from 542 to 488 million years ago. Most of the main animal groups evolved in this period.

**Camouflage** Colors or patterns that help an animal to blend in with its surroundings.

**Carnivore** An animal that eats only meat.

**Cenozoic** The era of time that followed the Mesozoic. It began 65 million years ago and extends up to the present day. Cenozoic literally means "new animal life."

**Ceratopsians** A group of four-legged, horned, plant-eating ornithischian dinosaurs, such as *Triceratops,* with a bony frill at the back of the skull.

**CGI** Short for computer-generated imagery, CGI is any illustration created using a computer, including 3-D models and animation sequences.

**Cold-blooded** Describes an animal whose body temperature rises and falls along with the temperature of its surroundings.

**Colony** A group of separate individuals working together, as in an ant or bird colony, or animals joined by strands of living tissues as in the case of corals.

**Coniferous** Cone-bearing trees, such as pine or fir.

**Coprolite** Fossilized dung of a animal.

**Cretaceous Period** The third period of the Mesozoic Era, lasting from 145 to 65 million years ago. An asteroid or comet hit Earth at the end of this period, triggering the demise of the dinosaurs.

**Crocodilians** The group that includes living crocodiles and alligators and their immediate ancestors. They and their extinct relatives are known as the crocodilomorphs and belong to the archosaur group of reptiles.

**Crurotarsans** A group of archosaurs that included the crocodilomorphs and other related reptiles, such as the rauisuchians and aetosaurs.

**Cycad** A tropical or subtropical plant that bears its seeds in large cones, but has a crown of leaves like a tree fern or palm.

**Cynodonts** A group of mammal-like reptiles with mammal-like teeth, which include canines, incisors, and molars. They included the ancestors of mammals.

**Dicynodonts** A group of plant-eating mammal-like reptiles with two tusks and a blunt beak.

**Dinosaurs** A group of archosaurs that evolved in the Triassic Period and dominated life on land in the Jurassic until they went extinct at the end of the Cretaceous. The birds are their direct descendants.

**Ecosystem** A collection of organisms living together in the same habitat, together with their environment.

**Embryo** An animal or plant in an early stage of development from an egg or a seed.

**Environment** The natural surroundings in which an animal or plant lives.

**Era** A unit of time that is further divided into periods.

**Evolution** The gradual change in living organisms that occur over many generations. Evolution may result in new species. Dinosaurs evolved from archosaur ancestors and birds evolved from feathered theropods.

**Extinction** The dying out of a plant or animal species. Extinction can happen naturally as a result of competition between species, changes in the environment, natural disasters (such as an asteroid or comet striking the Earth), or other factors.

**Ferns** A group of nonflowering plants that reproduce by spores rather than by seeds.

**Fossil** The remains of a dead organism, preserved in rock. Teeth and bones are more likely to form fossils than softer body parts, such as muscles and internal organs.

**Fossilization** The process by which dead organisms turn into fossils.

**Genus (plural, Genera)** In the classification of living organisms, a group of closely related species. The theropod *Tyrannosaurus rex* belongs to the genus *Tyrannosaurus*.

**Ginkgo** One of a group of nonflowering plants that grows into a tall tree with triangular leaves.

**Gondwana** One of the two continents that Pangaea split into at the end of the Triassic Period.

**Gymnosperms** One of the two main types of land plant that produce seeds. This group includes cycads, ginkgos, and conifers, such as pine and fir.

**Hadrosaurs** A group of large, bipedal and quadrupedal ornithopods from the Late Cretaceous Period known as duck-billed dinosaurs. They had a ducklike bill and fed on plants.

**Herbivore** An animal that eats only plants.

**Hominids** A group of primate mammals that includes humans, chimpanzees, and gorillas, together with their extinct close relatives. It does not include orangutans, gibbons, and monkeys.

**Hypsilophodonts** A group of fast-moving, bipedal ornithopods.

**Ichthyosaurs** A group of dolphinlike, predatory marine reptiles that were common in the Mesozoic Era. They had large eyes, pointed heads, and sharklike fins and tails.

**Iguanodonts** A group of ornithopod dinosaurs that ranged from small to large. They all had horselike faces. The group was named after an ornithopod called *Iguanodon*.

**Invertebrate** An animal without a backbone.

**Jurassic Period** The second period of the Mesozoic Era, lasting from 200 to 145 million years ago. During the Jurassic Period, dinosaurs dominated the land, the first birds evolved, and mammals began to spread out.

**Keelbone** The enlarged, deepened breastbone of a bird that anchors the large flight muscles. All modern birds have one, but some early birds did not.

**Keratin** The substance that forms skin, hair, horns, and nails or hooves of an animal.

**Laurasia** One of the two continents that were formed after Pangaea split at the end of the Triassic.

**Lava** The molten rock expelled by an erupting volcano or the solid rock that forms after cooling.

**Mammals** A group of warm-blooded vertebrates that feed their young on milk and whose skin is covered in hair or fur. Mammals evolved from cynodont ancestors in the Triassic Period.

**Mesozoic Era** The era lasting from 252 to 65 million years ago, containing the Triassic, Jurassic, and Cretaceous periods.

**Metriorhynchids** A family of fierce, marine crocodilian predators that had a streamlined body.

**Mollusks** A large group of invertebrate species including slugs, snails, clams, octopuses, and squid. Many mollusks produce hard shells that fossilize easily, making mollusk fossils common.

**Mosasaurs** A group of large aquatic lizards with paddle-shaped limbs and a tail flattened from side to side. They hunted fish and other marine creatures in the Cretaceous Period.

**Nesting colony** A colony of animals, such as birds and dinosaurs, that is formed when the animals gather in the same area to build nests and care for their eggs and young.

**Nodosaurs** A group of four-legged, armored, plant-eating dinosaurs that had bony plates on their backs and spines on the sides. They were related to the ankylosaurs.

**Nothosaurs** A group of predatory reptiles that lived in the Triassic seas. They had four legs with webbed feet and may have bred on shores like seals.

**Omnivore** An animal that eats both plants and other animals.

**Ornithischians** One of the two main dinosaur groups. In ornithischians, the pelvis (hip bone) was arranged as in a bird. Ornithischians included stegosaurs, ankylosaurs, ceratopsians, ornithopods, and pachycephalosaurs.

**Ornithomimids** A group of theropods that resembled ostriches. They were known as ostrich dinosaurs.

**Ornithopods** A group of plant-eating, mainly bipedal, ornithischians with long hind limbs. This group includes the hypsilophodonts, iguanodonts, and hadrosaurs.

**Oviraptorosaurs** A group of theropods with parrotlike skulls and feathered bodies.

**Pachycephalosaurs** A group of bipedal dinosaurs with thick, domed skulls.

**Paleontologist** A scientist who studies the fossil remains of plants and animals.

**Paleontology** The scientific study of fossilized plants and animals.

**Paleozoic** The era of time that came before the Mesozoic Era. It lasted from 542 to 252 million years ago. Paleozoic means "ancient animal life."

**Pangaea** The supercontinent that existed in the Paleozoic and Mesozoic eras.

**Period** A unit of time that is a division of an era—the Triassic Period is part of the Mesozoic Era.

**Pigments** Chemicals that give color to an organism. Giving color may be the main function of the pigment or the coloration may be incidental.

**Placenta** The organ that forms inside a pregnant mammal partly from the embryo and partly from the wall of the mother's womb, or uterus. The placenta allows exchange of nutrients and waste between the mother and developing young of placental mammals. *Eomaia* was one of the first placental mammals.

**Plesiosaurs** A group of meat-eating sea reptiles from the Jurassic and Cretaceous periods that swam in the seas using flipperlike limbs. Many had a snakelike neck and a small head.

**Pliosaurs** A group of plesiosaurs that had a short muscular neck and a large head with crocodilelike teeth. They were among the most formidable of all marine predators.

**Precambrian** The time between the formation of the Earth and the beginning of the Cambrian Period.

**Predator** An animal that hunts, kills, and eats other animals for food.

**Primates** A group of mammals that includes lemurs, monkeys, apes, and humans.

**Primitive** At an early stage of evolution.

**Prosauropods** A group of early, mainly plant-eating saurischian dinosaurs. They were the ancestors of the giant, long-necked sauropods.

**Psittacosaurs** A group of bipedal ceratopsians from the Cretaceous Period. Psittacosaurs had deep, parrotlike beaks that they used to eat plants.

**Pterosaurs** A group of archosaur reptiles that were capable of powered flight. They had batlike wings made of skin. Some of these were the largest creatures ever to fly.

**Pubis** One of the three bones that forms the pelvis of an animal.

**Quadrupedal** Describes an animal that walks on four limbs.

**Rauisuchians** A group of archosaur reptiles with upright limbs that lived in the Triassic. Many rauisuchians were dinosaurlike.

**Reptile** A group of cold-blooded vertebrates with scaly skin that typically live on land and reproduce by laying eggs. Lizards, snakes, turtles, and crocodiles are reptiles.

**Saurischians** One of the two main dinosaur groups. In saurischians, the pelvis was arranged as in a lizard. Saurischians include the predatory theropods and the sauropodomorphs.

**Sauropodomorphs** A group of plant-eating saurischians, including the prosauropods and sauropods.

**Sauropods** A group of gigantic, long-necked saurischians that included some of the largest animals ever to walk on the Earth.

**Scutes** Bony plates with a covering made of horn, set in the skin of certain reptiles. Scutes help form body armor in these reptiles.

**Sediment** Material such as sand and mud deposited by wind, water, or ice.

**Serrated** Saw-toothed, like a steak knife.

**Skull** The head's bony framework that protects the brain, eyes, ears, and nasal passages.

**Stegosaurs** A group of four-legged, plant-eating ornithischian dinosaurs with rows of tall bony plates and spines running down their backs and tails.

**Stromatolites** Large, hard, domelike structures in shallow seawaters, made of thin layers of particles built up by the action of generations of microorganisms, such as cyanobacteria. Stromatolites were very common in Precambrian times.

**Temperate** Describes a climate that is neither very hot nor very cold.

**Territory** The part of an animal's habitat that it defends from rival animals, usually of its own species.

**Tetrapods** Vertebrates with four limbs (arms, legs, or wings). All amphibians, reptiles, mammals, and birds are tetrapods. All tetrapods evolved from a fishlike ancestor.

**Theropods** A group of meat-eating dinosaurs. All theropods were predatory. They typically had sharp teeth and claws and ranged in size from the tiny *Microraptor* to the colossal *Tyrannosaurus*.

**Trace fossils** The signs of prehistoric creatures or their activities rather than remains of the creatures themselves, preserved in rock. Trace fossils include footprints, bite marks, droppings, and eggs.

**Triassic Period** The first period of the Mesozoic Era, lasting from 252 to 200 million years ago. Dinosaurs evolved in the Triassic Period.

**Tropical** Describes the region that spans the equator. It is a hot region with plenty of rainfall, resulting in the growth of tropical rainforests.

**Tyrannosaurids** A group of large theropods with short arms and two-fingered hands. They were named after *Tyrannosaurus*.

**Vertebrae** The bones that make up the backbone, or spine, of an animal.

**Vertebrates** Animals with a spinal column, or backbone.

**Warm-blooded** Describes an animal that maintains a constant internal body temperature. Mammals and birds are warm-blooded and at least some dinosaurs were, too. Their body temperature does not change with the temperature of their surroundings.

**Wingspan** The distance from the tip of one wing of an animal to the tip of the other when both wings are outstretched.

# Index

# QR

Quaternary Period 7
*Quetzalcoatlus* 134–5, 140, 142
rauisuchians 108–9, 112–13
reconstruction 30–1
records, prehistoric 142–3
Reichenbach, Ernest Stromer von 146
reptiles 5, 14, 15, 143
*Rhabdodon* 90
*Rhamphorhynchus* 136–7
*Rhomaleosaurus* 129, 130–1
rhynchosaurs 9, 103, 104–5
*Rhynchosaurus* 104–5
Riggs, Elmer S. 146

# S

*Saltasaurus* 66–7
saurischians 17, 146
*Saurolophus* 145
*Sauropelta* 79
sauropodomorphs 17
sauropods 6, 11, 16, 17, 60–71, 144
*Sauroposeidon* 142, 144
*Scelidosaurus* 74–5
*Scutellosaurus* 72
sea reptiles 10, 118–32, 143
Seeley, Harry Govier 146
*Shangtungosaurus* 142, 145
*Shonisaurus* 124, 143
*Shunosaurus* 70
*Simosuchus* 111
*Sinoconodon* 117
*Sinornithosaurus* 18, 27
*Sinosauropteryx* 18, 147
*Sinraptor* 43

skeletons 24, 25, 30
skin, fossilized 23, 26
skulls
    fossil 25
    largest/thickest 142
*Sphenosuchus* 88–9, 110
spines and spikes 16, 72, 78, 97
*Spinosaurus* 41, 145, 146
*Stagonolepis* 106
*Stegoceras* 96
stegosaurs 17, 72–7
*Stegosaurus* 73, 147
stromatolites 4
*Styracosaurus* 17, 101
*Suchomimus* 40
*Supersaurus* 144

# T

tails 80, 83, 136–7
*Tarbosaurus* 44–5
teeth 16, 56, 114, 142
*Temnodontosaurus* 125
*Tempskya* 12
*Tenontosaurus* 86–7
*Terrestrisuchus* 110
tetrapods 5, 14
*Thecodontosaurus* 57
theropods 6, 11, 17, 18, 19, 36–53, 145
*Thrinaxodon* 115
*Titanosaurus* 66
trace fossils 23, 28–9
Triassic Period 6, 8–9, 34, 116
*Triceratops* 13, 98, 99, 146, 147
*Troodon* 50–1, 142, 147
*Tsintaosaurus* 147
*Tuojiangosaurus* 77

*Tupandactylus* 141, 142
*Turiasaurus* 144
turtles 119, 120–1
tusks 114
*Tyrannosaurus* 36, 46–7, 145, 146
*Tyrannotitan* 145

# UVW

*Ultrasaurus* 142
*Umoonasaurus* 143
*Vegavis* 55
*Velociraptor* 51, 146
vertebrae 142
vertebrates 4, 5
volcanic activity 20, 21
*Vulcanodon* 63
*Westlothiana* 14
*Williamsonia* 10

# XYZ

*Xiaotingia* 54, 143
*Xiphactinus* 23
Yang Zhongjian 147
*Zalambdalestes* 13
Zhen Shou-nan 147
*Zhuchengtyrannus* 145

# Ackn

Dorling Kindersley would like to than[...]
Wild for proofreading; Helen Peters [...]
David Roberts and Rob Campbell fo[...]
creation; Claire Bowers, Fabian Harr[...]
Werblow, and Rose Horridge for DK [...]
Library Assistance; Tanveer Abbas 2[...]
CTS assistance; and Tanya Mehrotri[...]
Mahipal Singh for design assistance[...]

[...]ndersley: Peter Minister,
[...]or (br); Royal Tyrrell Museum
[...]ogy, Alberta, Canada (tr). 96
[...]ersley: Royal Tyrrell Museum
[...]ogy, Alberta, Canada (br). 97
[...]us Images (background). Dorling
[...]Peter Minister, Digital Sculptor.
[...]ndersley: Natural History Museum,
[...]cl, br, tl). 99 Corbis: Inspirestock

The publishers would also like to thank
the following for their kind permission
to reproduce their photographs:

(Key: a-above; b-below/bottom; c-centre; f-far;
l-left; r-right; t-top)

1 Dorling Kindersley: Peter Minister, Digital
Sculptor (c). 2–3 Dorling Kindersley: Jon
Hughes (c). 4 naturepl.com: Doug Perrine (bl).
6–7 Science Photo Library: MARK GARLICK
(bc). 6 Dorling Kindersley: Jon Hughes (r).
7 Getty Images: Dan Kitwood (tr). 8 Dorling
Kindersley: Andy Crawford / David Donkin -
modelmaker (tl). 9 Dorling Kindersley: Jon
Hughes (ca); Peter Minister, Digital Sculptor
(br). 10 Dorling Kindersley: Andy Crawford /
David Donkin - modelmaker (tl). 11 Dorling
Kindersley: Andrew Kerr (b); Peter Minister,
Digital Sculptor (tl). Getty Images: Siri Stafford /
Riser (b/background). 12 Dorling Kindersley:
Andy Crawford / David Donkin - modelmaker
(tl). 13 Corbis: Inspirestock (br/background).
Dorling Kindersley: Peter Minister, Digital
Sculptor (br). 14 Dorling Kindersley: Natural
History Museum, London (b); The Oxford
University Museum of Natural History (cr). 16
Dorling Kindersley: Peter Minister, Digital
Sculptor (bl). 17 Dorling Kindersley: Tim Ridley
/ Robert L. Braun - modelmaker (bl). 18 Corbis:
Grant Delin / Outline Gallery (bc). Reuters: Mike
Segar (r). 19 Dorling Kindersley: Peter Minister,
Digital Sculptor (cr). Science Photo Library:
Christian Darkin (tl). 20 Science Photo Library:
MARK GARLICK (b). 21 Alamy Images: Yogesh
More / ephotocorp (cl). Dorling Kindersley:
Bedrock Studios / Jon Huges (br). Science
Photo Library: D. Van Ravenswaay (tl). 23
Dorling Kindersley: James Stevenson /
Donks Models - modelmaker (bl). 24 Dorling
Kindersley: Natural History Museum, London.
25 Dorling Kindersley: Royal Tyrrell Museum of
Palaeontology, Alberta, Canada (tr). 26 Dorling
Kindersley: Natural History Museum, London
(bl). The Natural History Museum, London: (tr).
27 Reuters: Mike Segar (r). 29 Corbis: Louie
Psihoyos / Terra (tr). Dorling Kindersley: Natural
History Museum, London (bl). 30 Corbis: Louie
Psihoyos / Terra. 32 Corbis: Philippe Widling /
Design Pics (background). Dorling Kindersley:
Peter Minister, Digital Sculptor. 33 Corbis: Kevin
Schafer (br/background). Dorling Kindersley:
Peter Minister, Digital Sculptor (br). 36 Corbis:
Randall Levensaler Photography / Aurora Photos
(br/Background). Dorling Kindersley: Natural
History Museum, London (tl); Peter Minister,
Digital Sculptor (br). 38–39 Corbis: Philippe
Widling / Design Pics (background). Dorling

46–47 Corbis: Randall Levensaler Photography /
Aurora Photos (bc/background). Dorling
Kindersley: Peter Minister, Digital Sculptor (c).
47 Dorling Kindersley: Natural History Museum,
London (br). 48 Dorling Kindersley: Royal
Tyrrell Museum of Palaeontology, Alberta,
Canada (b). 48–49 Dorling Kindersley: Royal
Tyrrell Museum of Palaeontology, Alberta,
Canada (tc). 49 Corbis: Owen Franken (r/
background). Dorling Kindersley: Peter
Minister, Digital Sculptor (r). 50 Science Photo
Library: Christian Darkin (b). 51 Dorling
Kindersley: Jon Hughes (bl); Peter Minister,
Digital Sculptor (br). 52–53 Corbis: Owen
Franken (background). Dorling Kindersley:
Peter Minister, Digital Sculptor. 54 Corbis:
moodboard (b/background). Dorling
Kindersley: Peter Minister, Digital Sculptor
(b). 55 Dorling Kindersley: Jon Hughes (bl);
Natural History Museum, London (tc); Peter
Minister, Digital Sculptor (tl). 56 Dorling
Kindersley: Jon Hughes (br); Institute of
Geology and Palaeontology, Tubingen, Germany
(cl, bl). 61 Alamy Images: Rob Walls (tl). Corbis:
Louie Psihoyos / Science Faction (tr). 62–63
Dorling Kindersley: Peter Minister, Digital
Sculptor (r). Getty Images: Siri Stafford / Riser
(t/background). 62 Getty Images: Jeffrey L.
Osborn / National Geographic (br). 64–65
Dorling Kindersley: Peter Minister, Digital
Sculptor. Getty Images: Siri Stafford / Riser
(background). 66–67 Corbis: Alan Traeger
(b/background). Dorling Kindersley: Peter
Minister, Digital Sculptor (b). 66 Dorling
Kindersley: Jon Hughes (b). 68–69 Dorling
Kindersley: Andrew Kerr. Getty Images: Siri
Stafford / Riser (r/background). 68 Dorling
Kindersley: Jon Hughes (l). 70 The Natural
History Museum, London: (br). 73 Dorling
Kindersley: Peter Minister, Digital Sculptor.
Getty Images: Holger Spiering (background).
74–75 Dorling Kindersley: Peter Minister,
Digital Sculptor. Getty Images: Oliver Strewe /
Photographer's Choice (background). 77
Dorling Kindersley: Leicester Museum (r). 80
Dorling Kindersley: Jon Hughes (b). 82–83
Corbis: John Carnemolla (background). Dorling
Kindersley: Peter Minister, Digital Sculptor. 84
Corbis: Kevin Schafer (br/background). Dorling
Kindersley: Peter Minister, Digital Sculptor (br).
85 Corbis: Paul A. Souders (t/background).
Dorling Kindersley: Peter Minister, Digital
Sculptor (t). 88–89 Corbis: Paul A. Souders
(background). Dorling Kindersley: Peter
Minister, Digital Sculptor. 91 Dorling
Kindersley: Jon Hughes. 94–95 Dorling
Kindersley: Peter Minister, Digital Sculptor.
Getty Images: Panoramic Images (background).

(br/background). 100–101 Getty Images:
De Agostini Picture Library (tc). 104–105
Dorling Kindersley: Institute of Geology and
Palaeontology, Tubingen, Germany (b). 105
Dorling Kindersley: Natural History Museum,
London (t). 107 Dorling Kindersley: Jon Hughes
(br). 108 Dorling Kindersley: Jon Hughes (tl).
114 Dorling Kindersley: Natural History
Museum, London (cl). 115 Dorling Kindersley:
Natural History Museum, London (bl). 122
Dorling Kindersley: Royal Tyrrell Museum
of Palaeontology, Alberta, Canada (bl). 123
Dorling Kindersley: David Peart (background).
125 Dorling Kindersley: Jon Hughes (b). 126
Dorling Kindersley: Hunterian Museum
(University of Glasgow) (b). 129 Corbis: Mark A.
Johnson (tr/background). Dorling Kindersley:
Peter Minister, Digital Sculptor (tr). 130–131
Corbis: Mark A. Johnson (background). Dorling
Kindersley: Peter Minister, Digital Sculptor.
135 Dorling Kindersley: Peter Minister, Digital
Sculptor (bc). 136 Dorling Kindersley: Jon
Hughes (tl). 137 Dorling Kindersley: Jon
Hughes (bl); Peter Minister, Digital Sculptor
(tr); Robert L. Braun - modelmaker (br). Getty
Images: DAJ (tr/background). 138–139 Dorling
Kindersley: Peter Minister, Digital Sculptor.
Getty Images: DAJ (background). 141 Dorlin[...]
Kindersley: Peter Minister, Digital Sculptor

Jacket images: Front: Dorling Kindersley:
The American Museum of Natural History c
Graham High at Centaur Studios - modelm
tl, cr/ (Brachiosaurus), cb, Jon Hughes tr, cu
(Argentinosaurus), bl/ (Velociraptor), Jon Hug
/ Bedrock Studios ftr, tl/ (Scutosaurus), cla,
Graham High - modelmaker tl/ (Pentaceratops),
Jonathan Hately - modelmaker cra/ (Baryonyx),
Robert L. Braun - modelmaker ca, cra/
(Dilophosaurus), crb/ (Carnotaurus), br,
Centaur Studios - modelmakers c/ (Triceratops),
Leicester Museum clb/ (Tuojiangosaurus),
Natural History Museum, London crb/
(Archaeopteryx), bl, bl/ (Psittacosaurus), br/
(Triceratops), Peter Minister, Digital Sculptor bl/
(Deinonychus), c, Tim Ridley / Robert L. Braun
- modelmaker bl/ (Styracosaurus), Royal Tyrrell
Museum of Palaeontology, Alberta, Canada tr/
(skeleton), cr, crb; Back: Dorling Kindersley:
Jon Hughes fclb, Jonathan Hately - modelmaker
clb, Royal Tyrrell Museum of Palaeontology,
Alberta, Canada cla; Spine: Dorling Kindersley:
Peter Minister, Digital Sculptor t.

All other images © Dorling Kindersley

For further information see:
www.dkimages.com